THE AUGSBURG RAID

By the same author:

LANCASTER TARGET (ppb)
MOSQUITO VICTORY (ppb)

THE AUGSBURG RAID

The story of one of the most
dramatic and dangerous raids
ever mounted by RAF Bomber Command

JACK CURRIE DFC

GOODALL PUBLICATIONS LTD
London and St. Albans

First published in 1987 by
Goodall Publications Ltd

Front Cover: From an oil painting by Peter Coombs

Design: Peter Gunthorpe

GOODALL PUBLICATIONS LTD
London and St. Albans
Photo typesetting by Brian Robinson, Buckingham
Made and printed in Great Britain by
Robert Hartnoll (1985) Ltd., Bodmin, Cornwall
ISBN 0 907579 09 4

Contents

Caption to pages 6 and 7

Pages one and two of the famous Bomber Command Operation Order No. 143 directing the daylight attack by Lancasters on the M.A.N. diesel factory at Augsburg.

Crown copyright material in the Public Record Office is reproduced by permission of the Controller of Her Majesty's Stationery Office. (Ref. AIR 16/757)

Caption to pages 142 and 143

The recommendations for the Victoria Cross for S/Ldr. J. D. Nettleton, No 44 Squadron and S/Ldr. J. S. Sherwood, DFC & Bar, No. 97 Squadron. S/Ldr. Nettleton deservedly received his VC but in the case of S/Ldr. Sherwood, although recommended for the VC by the C-in-C Bomber Command, Air Marshal Harris, his papers were endorsed, 'To be recd for DSO if later found to be alive'. S/Ldr. Sherwood became a POW and in fact was awarded the DSO instead of the VC. (*See page 104*)

Crown copyright material in the Public Record Office is reproduced by permission of the Controller of Her Majesty's Stationery Office. (Ref. AIR 2/5686)

AIR 16/757.

/A

Copy No: 4

Date : 8th April, 1942.

INFORMATION.

1.   It is known that the present strength of the G.A.F. in fighter aircraft is, in spite of feverish efforts to recuperate, at a lower figure than it was a year ago. Notwithstanding urgent calls for more fighters in other theatres of war the enemy has had to maintain a considerabl fighter force on the western front. This force however has necessarily had to be deployed over a length of coastline exceeding 2,000 miles. Apart from the temporary concentration in Norway, the bulk of these day fighters on the Western Front are disposed in the PAS DE CALAIS area. Other coastal areas are, as a result, covered only with meagre fighter forces and inland areas are still less covered. What units there are in these areas have frequently been found inferior in ability and determination to the units in the PAS DE CALAIS area. The majority of fighter units in the sparsely covered areas are night fighters, and they are disposed almost exclusively in N.W. Germany and Holland.

2.   The heavy bomber carries a powerful defensive armament, it is capable of comparatively high speeds and it has a long range. Operating in daylight the fire power of a section of three heavy bombers is such as to deter all but the most determined of enemy fighters. Its speed provides the enemy with a difficult interception problem. Its range enables it to outflank the enemy defences and to strike deep into the Southern interior of Germany.

3.   The combination of the qualities of the heavy bomber with well co-ordinated diversions should, therefore, enable a force of heavy bombers to cross the coast of France in daylight at a weak point and to penetrate deep inland without meeting serious opposition. By this means vital targets hitherto not attacked owing to the difficulty of location at night or on account of the distance involved, can be attacked with comparative precision. By making the attack at dusk the return journey can be made under cover of darkness.

4.   A daylight attack on an important industry in a town hitherto unmolested by bombing either by day or by ight should cause considerable alarm and despondency among the population who at present may consider themselves outside the danger area.

INTENTION.

5.   To attack the M.A.N. Diesel Factory at AUGSBURG (G.R.3680) in daylight.

EXECUTION,

Code Name.

6.   This operation will be known by the code name
MARGIN.

Outline Plan.

7.   Six Lancaster aircraft of No.5 Group will
constitute the heavy bomber force. The aircraft will fly
in two sec. ons of three in company until forced to
separate by darkness. (See para.8 below).

Route.

8.   The force will be routed to the target as
follows, the latter half of the route being so designed
as to indicate to the enemy that MUNICH is the objective.

```
SELSEY BILL
DIVES SUR MER   (49°22'N, 00°06'W)
SENS            (48°11'N, 03°15'E)
LUDWIGSHAFEN    (47°50'N, 09°03'E)
AMIEN SEE       (48°03'N, 11°04'E)
TARGET.
```

Towns and defended areas should be avoided on the outward
route.   The return route will be direct from target to
home base unless the remaining period of daylight necessi-
tates a withdr. wal. to the South West until there is sufficient cover from darkness.

Method of Attack.

9.   After reaching the northern end of AMMER SEE the
formation will turn left handed and reducing height will
head straight for the target. The attack will be carried
out at a low level by each section independently.

Bomb Load.

10.   Each aircraft is to carry maximum 1,000 lb. G.I.
Bombs filled R.D.X. fused T.D. 11 secs.

Heights.

11.   The force will fly below 500 ft. after leaving
the English coast until south of Paris in order to avoid
detection by R.D.F. The remainder of the journey to the
target will be carried out at heights most suitable
tactically under the prevailing conditions. It should be
borne in mind that flying at ground level presents the
most difficult problem to the attacking fighters.

12.   Full details of the target will be forwarded to
No.5 Group by Intelligence.

7

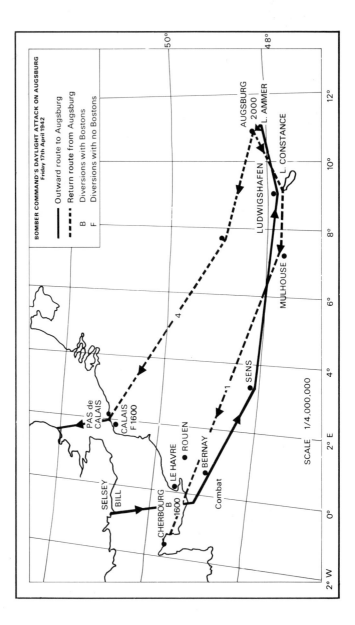

BOMBER COMMAND'S DAYLIGHT ATTACK ON AUGSBURG
Friday 17th April 1942

—— Outward route to Augsburg
---- Return route from Augsburg
B   Diversions with Bostons
F   Diversions with no Bostons

50°

48°

12°

AUGSBURG
2000

L. AMMER

LUDWIGSHAFEN

L. CONSTANCE

MULHOUSE

4

SENS

PAS de
CALAIS

CALAIS
F 1600

6°

ROUEN

BERNAY

Combat

SELSEY
BILL

LE HAVRE

CHERBOURG
B
1600

SCALE 1/4,000,000

2° E

0°

2° W

1

Foreword

When the war was over (World War II, that is) I stayed on in the RAF, sometimes flying aeroplanes, sometimes flying desks. One of the flying appointments was with No 44 (Rhodesia) Squadron at Wyton, in Huntingdonshire, where we flew the Avro Lincoln, a later, slightly bigger version of that Queen of aeroplanes, the Lancaster – bigger, and considerably clumsier. As a Flight Commander, I was treading in some famous footsteps, including those of the man who led the Augsburg raid in 1942. I don't remember thinking much about that at the time; in fact, I don't remember that we talked at all of Augsburg on the Squadron then. Perhaps it was too close to the event, in 1948, to get it in perspective – like standing so close to a painting that you can't quite take it in. Now, we're far enough away to have a better view, and I'm grateful to the publisher for giving me the chance.

I also want to thank some others who have helped along the way: Ian McBride of Easingwold, ex-RAF himself, who took over much of the research when David Shackleton was tragically killed in a flying accident: Jim MacDonald of the Wickenby Register, who found important documents in The Public Record

Office: Harold Piper, veteran flight engineer, whose memory for Lancaster detail is like a technical library: Alan Cooper, the RAF historian, who led me to the expert in Luftwaffe records, Werner Gerbig: the BBC archivists who unearthed the tapes of what was said on radio about the raid: the Air Historical Branch of the Ministry of Defence, for their invariable help. I have been allowed to use research material from two splendid books – 'Bomber Command' and 'The Fall of Fortresses' – and for that I thank, respectively, the authors Max Hastings and Elmer Bendiner DFC (himself an ex-USAAF bomber man). I am indebted to two ex-members of the Women's Auxiliary Air Force: Mrs 'Pip' Brimson, who served at Waddington in 1942, and Mrs Betty Nettleton, who told me aspects of the story only she could know about.

For their contributions to the story, special thanks must go to the Augsburgers themselves: Erika Harbacher, Karl Dömling, Albert Fackler (who was badly wounded in the brave but ill-starred seaborne raid, largely by Canadian soldiers, on Dieppe in August 1942, five months after the action of this story), Karl-Heinz Meinecke, Johann Wagner and the late Lukas Kiermeyr, who died peacefully in Augsburg in 1984. They recounted their experiences and their feeling with much humanity and warmth; Madeleine Harcourt-Leftwich translated and put her heart into the work.

For some historic photographs, gratitude is due to the directors of M.A.N. – the great Augsburg factory which was the bombers' target.

There is an occasional piece of conversation in this book, and I know some critics don't like that in histories. They'll call it 'faction', and they'll think I've made it up. Well, so I have – but mostly from what people who were on the scene have told me. And when it comes to airmen talking to each other, it's true I have imagined some of that, because I do recall the feelings, and the language.

Lastly and chiefly, I am grateful to those surviving heroes of the raid who shared their memories with Ian or with me: Wing Commanders David Penman OBE DSO DFC, Brian Hallows OBE DFC, Edward Rodley DSO DFC, Squadron Leader Patrick Dorehill DSO DFC, Messrs Bertram Dowty (who makes a regular pilgrimage to his comrades' graves in Normandy and to certain gallant families of France), and Nichol Birkett. They do not need this book to honour them – honour enough is theirs – but I hope they like it.

1

Most Secret Operation Order No 143

The Minister of Information pushed back the lock of flame-red hair that often fell across his brow, and glanced round the conference room at the rows of cameramen and correspondents. 'These aircrews,' he said, pointing to the RAF men who sat on either side of him, 'flew over every clothes-line and chimney-pot in Europe to attack their target . . .' He excused himself the slight hyperbole: the phrase would make a headline for the list of decorations he had just announced.

A reporter put a question. The Minister referred it to the airman on his right. The airman rose – reluctantly, it seemed to those who watched – and cleared his throat. He was a well-built man in his middle twenties, dark-haired, with steady, deep-set eyes. His rank was Squadron Leader, his name John Deering Nettleton. Below the pilot's wings upon his tunic, he wore the dark-red ribbon of the Victoria Cross. His voice held no emotion, his careful accent no suggestion of his distant Cape Town home, as he admitted that his force had suffered heavy losses. 'Seven out of the twelve Lancasters that set out never came back . . .' He paused, head down. The pressmen leaned forward to catch the next few words. 'Five out of the seven belonged to my Squadron.' Nettleton squared his shoulders. 'The families of those who didn't come back may ask – was it worth the loss involved? My answer is – absolutely. All our fellows who returned were pretty confident that they had hit their target. And now we've got a report which shows that the M.A.N. factory was heavily damaged.' He paused again, with a glance at his companions. One of these, another pilot (who also wore a bright, new ribbon on his chest – that of the DFC), was quick to give support. 'I somehow don't think,' he said, with a flashing smile beneath the heavy, black moustache, 'that Jerry will be making any Diesel engines there for a long time to come.'

The Minister nodded. 'I happen to know Augsburg and the Diesel works well,' he said, as Nettleton gratefully resumed his seat, 'and I know what part they play in Germany's war effort . . .' To talk about an action that had not been a disaster was a very welcome change: he would have been a public man of superhuman reticence who failed to make the most of it. The previous month, March 1942, had been a diary of bad news. Rommel had recaptured Benghazi; the Japanese had swarmed into Rangoon and were landing in New Guinea; in the Atlantic, the U-boats had sent nearly half a million tons of Allied shipping to the bottom – a few more months like that and Britain would be starving. Even St. Nazaire, where at least the Navy had succeeded in blowing up the lock with the explosive-laden Campbeltown, had cost more than half the force of highly-trained Commandos – either killed or captured. The Minister was well aware of how despondent people were before the raid: the Institute of Public Opinion's

14

monthly check on satisfaction with the way the Government was managing the war had hit an all-time low of 35%, and the Home Office's intelligence reports, which measured popular reaction to events, had recorded 3 against a scale of 0 to 20, following the fall of Singapore. The Minister (whose name was Brendan Bracken) smiled round at the bomber men, and consented to be photographed among them.

A short bus ride away from the site of this event stood Adastral House – the main headquarters of the Air Ministry in London – where a certain Section Officer Havelock was going about her duties. She was a strikingly good-looking girl, twenty-one years old, and her appointment was that of PA to the Deputy Director of the Women's Auxiliary Air Force – the sort of job which sometimes came the way of young women officers who were properly brought-up, and blessed with both intelligence and charm. Betty Havelock had read about the raid on Augsburg in her daily paper, and admired the skill and courage of the aircrews. She decided that their leader, judging by the photograph, was an attractive man.

While cameras clicked and heroes smiled in London, six unshaven, weary men were waiting in a house – a so-called safe house – at La Trinité des Latiers, near Alençon in Normandy. They were a crew without a captain – he had left them, for good reason, when they had climbed out of their broken Lancaster ten days before – and they were weary because, although they had not travelled far in those ten days, the going had been hard. At least they were no longer hungry: the night before, Lucien Legenvre, whose home it was, and young Raymond, his son, had killed a pig for their regalement (the snails which were the first course of that feast they had politely but, so strong were Anglo-Saxon inhibitions, instinctively declined). They were waiting for a man called Francis Gagnard, once himself a pilot in the service of his country but now, since its fall, proprietor of an Alençon cafe. They had been told that he might help them on their way. The journey that they had in mind was difficult and long; it was a journey that would lead, they hoped, to England.

It was half a century since fortune had begun to smile on Rudolf Diesel. The year was 1892, the administration in Berlin had granted him a patent for his engine, and the Maschinenfabrik company had offered him, not only sponsorship, but the use of their great factory at Augsburg – his father's home, which also was his own for many years, once he had ceased to wander through the capitals of Europe, peddling his weird ideas of heat exchange. (That he was outspoken as a pacifist, a reformer of society, and a lover of the arts, had not always helped his credibility as a serious inventor.)

Next year, the engine ran, blew up – a chunk of metal missed Doktor Diesel's head by inches – and ran again. Within five years, he was a millionaire, his dream a reality – the heavy-duty engine, reliable in operation, needing no electric spark, using the cheapest grades of fuel, ideal for the workers of the world, for tractors, trucks and locomotives, for bulldozers and buses – and for submarines.

In 1913, Rudolf Diesel took the long train ride through Germany and France to visit England once again: no longer as a somewhat undesirable young alien, but to be honoured at an engineers' convention. On the

Channel ferry, he dined well with a companion and promptly disappeared. Opinion was that he fell overboard.

*   *   *

On Monday, 27th April 1942 (the day which saw the press reception for the aircrew who came home, and the vigil near Alençon of six men who did not), Lord Selborne, the Minister of Economic Warfare, wrote to Mr Winston Churchill. It was a rather sniffy letter. 'Dear Prime Minister,' it began, 'As it is part of my function to advise on economic objectives for air attack, I think that you should know the following facts about the Augsburg raid, which disturb me . . .' What disturbed Lord Selborne, as he went on to explain, was that his experts, in consultation with others at the Air Ministry, had picked, in order of priority, six economic targets for the bombers which they believed would hurt the Germans most. Diesel engine factories had not figured in the list, largely because there were so many of them around, in Germany and the occupied countries, that knocking out the odd one here or there would not do much good. It would have been far better to attack one of the recommended targets, like the fuel-pump factory at Stuttgart or the ball-bearing works at Schweinfurt, neither of which was all that far from Augsburg. The raid itself seemed to have been well enough conceived and carried out, but that was not the point. If Air Marshal Harris could send his bombers where he liked, ignoring all advice – that really was no way to run the war.

Sir Charles Portal, Chief of Air Staff, to whom

Winston Churchill passed this letter, took a different view. The selection of Augsburg as a target, he replied, had not been based on economic criteria alone. The Bomber C-in-C had taken tactical aspects into account for what had really been an experimental raid. Flying at low level, the crews had needed good landmarks for their run-in: Augsburg had them, Schweinfurt and Stuttgart did not. With the tiny force of Lancasters available, and no time to spare for searching round, the target had to be compact and easily identified: at Augsburg the factory was like that, those at Schweinfurt and Stuttgart were not. Furthermore, the C-in-C was keen to make some impact on the battle in the Atlantic, where the diesels powered the U-boats, and might not have felt inclined to get into a protracted wrangle with Lord Selborne's people as to how to do that best. There might also, the Chief of Air Staff hinted broadly, have been some concern in the C-in-C's mind about security at Lord Selborne's Economic Ministry. It would, however, be a good idea if the C-in-C discussed the economic value of his future targets with the Air Ministry, the Chief of Air Staff conceded, adding silkily, 'He has been so informed.'

Winston Churchill, playing piggy-in-the-middle, asked Lord Selborne if he wished to comment further. Indeed he did. For one thing, he was surprised to learn that, in selecting targets, the Bomber C-in-C had discretion to weigh such matters as the desirability of assisting in the Battle of the Atlantic: he had always supposed it was the job of the Defence Committee to decide that sort of thing. He took the point about the need for secrecy, and was confident that the arrangements he had made for passing information were secure.

As to the vulnerability of targets, and the effects of bombing damage on the enemy economy, he rather thought his Ministry had something to contribute. Briefly, Winston Churchill made response, remarking that he talked to both the Chief of Air Staff and Air Marshal Harris frequently. Perhaps Lord Selborne ought to try a similar approach – why not take Harris out to lunch? As to the target, the President of the USA had asked particularly for efforts against supply of U-boats. Incidentally, Lord Selborne should see 'this excellent reply from Air Marshal Harris to your paper.'

In this, the Bomber C-in-C examined all the arguments about the targets and the tactics, one by one, and laid them all to rest with hammer blows. 'But I could not in any circumstances,' ran his seventeenth paragraph, 'agree to discuss projected targets outside my Headquarters with other Departments. I do not even tell my crews, to whom security is a matter of life and death, where they are going until the last moment before briefing . . .'

Nineteen days before the press conference at the Information Ministry, and all that sniffy correspondence had begun, the Air Staff of Bomber Command, at their Headquarters on the hill above High Wycombe, had planned the operation – code-named 'Margin' – and Wing Commander Sam Elworthy had put it into writing. What he wrote, under headings of 'Information', 'Intention', 'Execution' and 'Administration' in best Staff College style, was designated Bomber Command Operation Order No 143 and classified 'Most Secret'. It was signed by Elworthy for the Senior Air Staff Officer at half-past six on the evening of April 8th, 1942 and taken by a motor-cyclist

19

of the Despatch Rider Letter Service to the Head-quarters of No 5 Bomber Group at Grantham – the Group whose Lancasters were to carry out the raid. Copies of the order went to No 2 Group HQ at Huntingdon (its Boston light bombers were to make diversionary attacks before the heavies crossed the coast), to Fighter Command HQ at Stanmore, and to the Fighter Groups whose Spitfires were to cover, and to help in, the diversions. All Headquarters were to acknowledge safe receipt by teleprinter.

Two squadrons only, at that time, had been equipped with Lancasters. One was No 44 (Rhodesia) Squadron at Waddington, three miles south of Lincoln, and the other was No 97 (Straits Settlements) Squadron at Woodhall Spa, twelve miles to the east. (Several squadrons had their numbers suffixed by an Empire title in recognition of colonial contributions to their strengths: Rhodesia, for example, had sent many men to join the ranks of 44 as air and ground crew, and the Squadron's crest – an elephant, above the motto 'Fulmina Regis Iusta' – recalled a Matabele king who, in Victoria's time, laid claim to being her 'thunderbolt' in his part of the world.)

The Lancaster had been developed from the Manchester, which had started life as A. V. Roe's response to an Air Ministry requirement, back in January 1937, for a heavy bomber to be built around two Rolls-Royce Vulture engines. It had taken four whole years to get the Manchester from drawing-board to service with the Squadrons, some of whose pilots (including those of 97 Squadron) would have gladly sent it back where it began. Then, with that element of luck which often marked a break-through in the air, the designers found the answer to their problem: the Vulture engine project had not turned out well and, although the Rolls-Royce Merlin had already proved a winner, two of them were not enough to lift the bomber's load. So Avro had conceived the Lancaster, utilising many of the Manchester's components, but with a whole new centre-section to accommodate four Merlins.

Within eight months – a brief enough gestation – the birth of the thirty-ton baby was being acclaimed. 'The aircraft is eminently suitable for operational duties,' the RAF's test report had stated. 'The performance and handling characteristics with full load surpass those of any other bomber. Even with two engines stopped on one side the performance is exceptional. Baulked landings present no difficulties, even with 60,000 lb loaded weight. Take-off and night landings are straight-forward. Manoeuvrability is good and evasive and jinking tactics easy.'

News of the baby had begun to spread along the pilots' grapevine. Late in 1941, it had reached 97 Squadron, and Flying Officer Rodley heard it for the first time in the crew-room. 'A type was telling me,' reported another pilot, 'that he'd seen a Manchester with four engines – going like a bat out of hell!' Edward Ernest Rodley was entirely typical of a commissioned bomber-pilot of the time. He had joined the RAFVR in 1937, as soon as he was old enough, learned to fly and practised at the weekends. At the threat of war, he had left his job with ICI and worn his uniform full time – no more an amateur, but still a volunteer. He had passed the Central Flying School course and flown as an instructor for a year or more until, at last, a posting

21

came for bombers. In the Mess at Finningley, his OTU, he had been met by a cherubic, pink-cheeked man who bought him beer and straightaway convinced him that Bomber Command was going to be a great deal more congenial than he had found Flying Training. (The pink-cheeked officer was Wing Commander Roderick Learoyd, known as 'Babe', who, flying low-level in a Hampden on 12th August, 1940, had destroyed a well-defended aqueduct of the Dortmund-Ems Canal, and earned the war's third air VC.) Rodley had passed through OTU, treating the Wellingtons – the ageing few that could be spared from operations – with every care, and moved on to Coningsby to fly the Manchester with 97 Squadron. His operational career had started on the 'nursery slopes' – short-range targets on the coast of France. He had failed to find Bordeaux and brought the bombs back home, as was encouraged by his frugal masters if not by the armourers whose task it was to take them off the aeroplane. Next time out, he had undergone, if not enjoyed, a salutary pelting by the guns of Dunkirk. By the time the Lancasters arrived, and 97 moved to Woodhall Spa, he had eight operations in his log-book, one of them by daylight, and well over a thousand hours of flying time as pilot. By comparison with the fledglings who would throng out of the training schools with 200 hours or so, to fly the Lancasters in 1943 and '44, he and the other bomber captains at Waddington and Woodhall were old hands.

The first batch of Lancasters had gone to Waddington, beginning on the Christmas Eve of '41, and the pilots had been learning how to fly them – teaching each other, for the most part – and had flown them through the teething troubles all new aircraft had, once the test-pilots had done with them and passed them to the real world – the rougher world – of squadron operation. At Waddington, Squadron Leader Nettleton had swung into a pile of frozen snow beside the runway and broken off his tail-wheel; Warrant Officer Crum and Sergeant Rhodes, on separate occasions, had not quite finished landing when they reached the runway's end. Like everyone who flew the Lancaster, they soon found out that, lightly loaded, it was an aeroplane that did not like to stall: it would float for ever if the speed were just a little bit too high.

No-one was in any doubt that the Lancaster was a vast improvement on the aged Hampdens and ill-conceived Manchesters with which they had been trying to prosecute the war ('Like a Rolls-Royce after an old Tin Lizzie', said Flight Lieutenant Penman of 97): nevertheless there was a tendency for quite important pieces to fall off the aeroplane. Flying Officer Deverill of 97, picking up a Lancaster from Boscombe Down, lost one of the main wheels, taking off, and an engine landed independently of the aircraft on a night detail at Coningsby (still 97's parent station). Rodley himself, loaded to the brim with petrol and six mines for the Frisian waters, tangled with low cloud soon after take-off and had to make a rather violent turn to miss the Boston roof-tops. At this, six feet of the starboard wing-tip disappeared, and the port tip folded upwards like a toilet seat. Slightly shaken, Rodley landed on the sands at Freiston, with the mines still in the bomb-bay. 'It shows which pieces break off first,' he commented, catching up his sprinting crew some hundred yards away, 'when you pull back hard.'

Wheels and engines falling off were no great problem:

they just had to be fixed on more securely. And, anyway, the Lancaster would fly quite well on only three of its great Merlins, and could be landed on its belly without great damage to the air-frame or trauma to the crew. But wing-tips breaking off was rather serious – serious enough for A. V. Roe to send their chief designer down to talk to Rodley. 'Did a wing-tip really break,' Roy Chadwick asked, 'or did you hit a chimney? I must know the truth.' Convinced, the experts went to Grantham for a chat. They had dinner with the 5 Group Tech. Staff men at the George Hotel and later, in the lounge, they pulled the carpet back for Harold Rogerson to chalk his answer to the problem on the floor. The Staff men drank their coffee and took note. The wings were modified, 97 took the air again, and 44 stopped calling them 'The 97th Foot'.

Their first operation with the Lancasters from Waddington had also been a mine-laying mission (known as 'Gardening'), in the Heligoland Bight on March 3rd – the sort of task that they had undertaken many times in Hampdens. The difference was that the Lancaster carried four of the great 'vegetables' to the Hampden's one, and could take them twice as far. Then came a proper bomber operation, against the steel town, Essen, in the Ruhr, but only two of 44's Lancasters could take part in that. The other eight were way up north at Lossiemouth, waiting for a chance to bomb the Tirpitz while she lurked in Fottenfiord, close by Trondheim, a constant threat to every Russian convoy. (The chance would come again for 44 at the end of April – the chance, but not the kill. That would be for 9 and 617 Squadrons, with their armour-piercing 'Tallboys', two and a half years later in the war.)

24

At Woodhall, too, 97's first real Lancaster attack, with HE and incendiaries, had been on Essen. Penman's observer, Flying Officer Ifould, had been unable to locate the target through the cloud, and Penman had continued south to bomb Cologne instead. Flight Sergeant Elwood, the mid-upper gunner, had called out: 'I've been hit!' A piece of shrapnel, fortunately spent, had struck him on the head. 'I expect it was quite painful,' Penman commented, 'but I thought he'd live.' (You could be hit by bits of flak some distance from the detonation point. They were formidable guns, the German 88s. They fired an 18 pound shell, usually in salvoes from a battery of four, and they could fire at five second intervals to a height, if required, of 27,000 feet. The shells were set to burst together in a piece of sky of sixty yards diameter, their lethal range was nearly half of that, and they caused some sort of damage up to 200 yards.)

It was when instructions came from HQ 5 Group to practice flying formation that they got an inkling of something strange being in the offing – strange in that their raids were mostly made by night, and you could not fly formation in the dark. Or could you? It might be possible by moonlight, or at dusk. Someone put the rumour round that they were to form a force of pathfinders; someone else that they were going to knock out gun positions on the coast of France, in preparation for a landing by the troops. A more cynical opinion was that it was all another whim of high command – like church parades for aircrew, or a route march round the airfield once a week. 'Never mind what it is,' said Sergeant Churchill, the wireless op in Nettleton's crew, 'it's keeping us off ops for a couple of weeks. That'll do me.'

25

'You and me both,' agreed his colleague. 'We can whoop it up in Lincoln every night.'

'Think what you like,' said Nettleton, 'but keep your mouths shut tight.' The practice routes grew longer, the formations tighter, and it became increasingly apparent that someone, somewhere, was planning to commit them to a daylight operation of some range. Formation flying started to make sense: the gunners, giving mutual support, would be far stiffer opposition for the Messerschmitts than one aircraft alone. That was the way, so they had heard, the USAAF meant to operate, once they began to get into the war.

Few of 44's or 97's pilots had flown serious formation since their days in training, and they had to work at it. Fortunately, the Lancaster was light on the controls, for all its size, and very stable in the air. They flew standard formation, nothing fancy, with two V-shaped sections of three aircraft each, the sections in line astern. Tagging along with the formations were two extra Lancasters, flying together 'in the box' behind a section leader or in echelon with No 2 or No 3. These, the aircrews understood, would stand by as reserves when the time came to fly the operation – whatever it might be.

Nettleton led the 44 formation, although he was a first tour pilot with only fifteen missions in his log book – far fewer than most of those who flew behind him. But he had already shown the qualities – the 'press-on spirit' as the aircrew called it – that gave him both the duty, and the right, to lead. And it happened that he had an empathy with those who faced the U-boats (although the relevance of this would not appear until the nature of the target was revealed), not only from a family

26

tradition – he had an Admiral for a grandfather – but from his own experience, for he had joined the Merchant Navy after leaving school in Cape Town, and served his time at sea. Then, while under training as a civil engineer, he had become a member of the RNVR, South African Division, and remained so until, in 1938, he had taken a commission in the RAF.

Sergeant George Rhodes flew in the Number Two position, on the right of Nettleton, and on the left, at Number Three, was Flying Officer Arthur Garwell, who had won the DFM as a non-commissioned pilot, and had so far flown two sorties of his second tour.

Flight Lieutenant Sandford, of Twickenham in Middlesex, led the second 'Vic' of 44. He was Reginald Robert Sandford to the Registrar of Births, and Nick to family and friends, but for something in his manner – perhaps the way he chose at times to stir them into action – his crew knew him as 'Flap'. At Numbers Two and Three respectively to Sandford were the tough, experienced Warrant Officers John Beckett and Hubert Crum – both holders of the DFM and bosom friends.

The 97 element was led by Squadron Leader Sherwood DFC, with Warrant Officer Harrison DFM and Flight Lieutenant Hallows as his wing-men, and Rodley as reserve. John Seymour Sherwood, born in Suez in the last year of the first World War, had taken his commission in 1937 and had earned the DFC on his first tour of operations. A bar had been added to that decoration in the previous December, when he had led 97's Manchesters in a daylight attack upon the Scharnhorst, the Gneisenau and the cruiser Prinz Eugen as they lay in dry dock at Brest. Brian Hallows, Sherwood's No 2 on that occasion and now his No 3, was still in single figures as to operations flown, but he had a lot of flying experience and had won a trophy for being 'Best all-round Cadet' at CFS. He had also won a reputation for the use of RT language which caused some Watchtower WAAFs to giggle, some to blush. He was known as 'Darkie' on the Squadron, not for his jet-black hair and full moustache, but for an episode, again when 97 flew the Manchesters, and when getting lost was less uncommon than it would become. Finding himself in this condition, Hallows had invoked the RT get-you-home service of those early days: 'Darkie, Darkie,' he had called. Receiving no response, he had tried again – still no reply. Once more, he had trans-mitted to the void: 'Darkie, Darkie . . . where are you, you little black bastard?'

Leading 97's second section was Flight Lieutenant David Jackson Penman. He had joined the RAF in 1937 straight from his Edinburgh school, had begun the war with 44, with whom he won the DFC, and now stood on the threshold of a tour with 97. Number Two to Penman was Warrant Officer Mycock – another who had won his DFC above the docks at Brest – while Flying Officer Ernest Alfred Deverill, from Gillingham in Dorset, flew at Number Three. Deverill, a 'Halton Brat' (or ex-aircraft apprentice), had remustered as a pilot in 1938 and flown more than a hundred sorties as a non-commissioned pilot – most of them in aircraft of Coastal Command. In May, 1940, his Hudson had been set upon by three Me 109s, one of which his gunners had shot down. With his rear gunner killed and his second pilot wounded, Deverill had flown his damaged aircraft home, and won the DFM.

When David Penman, as a pilot, had compared the

Lancaster with the Manchesters and Hampdens he had known, the Rolls-Royce simile was apt: his cushioned seat, with folding arm-rests, was as comfortable as any limousine. He could jack it up a bit (he was not a tall man), and set the rudder-pedals to the best position for his legs. Not for nothing was the cabin called 'the glasshouse', for the view was excellent ahead, to left and right, and up above. The wings were in the way of vision low on either beam, and the armour plate behind him made it hard to see astern, but he had the gunners to take care of those aspects. The mid-upper turret, half-way back along the fuselage, could turn through a full circle, and 'tail-end Charlie' covered everything that lay between the rudders (to prevent mid-upper gunners shooting holes in these or in the wings, deflecting blisters and arrester-bars would be installed as one of the Lancaster's first and, for the pilots, very welcome 'mods'.)

Penman's 'stick', with which he moved the ailerons and rudders, was not a stick at all – not like the joystick of a training aircraft or a fighter – but a substantial metal column with a double wheel (the 'spectacles') on top. The important levers, for the undercarriage, flaps and bomb-doors, were all conveniently placed, and the trim controls were also easy to locate and operate.

On Penman's right sat Pilot Officer Hooey, Canadian by birth and, at 33, ten years older than his captain. He had been a professional golfer in California when the war began, but had put aside his clubs 'for the duration' and taken ship for England to enlist. This next operation would be Hooey's fourth and, by all the signs, his second daylight, for he, too, had bombed the battleships Salmon and Gluckstein at Brest, and at low level, furthermore. Then, his aircraft had been badly damaged by the flak: whatever was to come would hold no fears – no new fears, anyway – for Gilbert Campbell Hooey.

His designation now was second pilot, but that was really a misnomer, a relic of the days when bombers had dual sets of the controls. None of the squadron Lancasters had these, and Hooey's role could be more accurately described as pilot's mate. The day, indeed, was shortly to arrive when the Command would have a Lancaster for every pilot, and a new breed of aircrew – a flight engineer – would take the 'second dickey' seat. It was a seat that was distinctly more austere than David Penman's: Hooey perched rather than sat upon a narrow, folding bench, and had nothing but a webbing strap on which to rest his back; even these simple fittings had to be dismantled, if another member of the crew, requiring access to the nose, was not prepared to crawl along the floor between his legs. Forward of the second pilot's station a step, which doubled as the cover of a glycol tank, led down into the nose compartment. It was there that Edward Lister Ifould, from Sydney, New South Wales, would man the Mark IX bombsight when required, lying prone upon the front escape-hatch, with the bomb release-tit in his hand. In that position, the movement of his head would be restricted by a flying-boot on either side of it, and in those boots would be the feet of Sergeant Tales, standing there to man the front gun-turret, with a pair of Browning .303s. All three turrets – made by Fraser-Nash – were hydraulically powered, and the pump for each was driven by a different engine, so that the failure of any one would not put all the gunners out of work.

Aft of Penman's armour-plated back-rest was Ifould's navigation 'office'. His seat faced to the port side of the cabin, on the inner frame of which were mounted the repeaters of such instruments – the altimeter, ASI and distant-reading compass – as observers had a need to know about. There, too, were set the screen and switches of the scientists' answer to a navigator's prayer – the Gee-box. (This device had only been in service for a month and, like all the observers, Ifould was still getting used to matching blips on his receiver with lines upon a map.) A desk, lit by an angled lamp, contained his log, Gee charts, Mercator maps and astro-navigation tables, and the desk-lid served him as a working surface. On the cabin's starboard side behind him, a blister window, shaped like half an egg, permitted him a view of ground beneath the aircraft – provided he could bend his neck at right angles – and rising from the aft end of the glasshouse was the astrodome, which would accommodate his sextant when he wanted to take star-shots for a fix. If he had cause to use the Gee in daylight, he could draw a black-out curtain right across the office, the better to identify the little pulses on the screen.

Immediately aft of Ifould's station, on the port side of the aircraft, sat Flight Sergeant Elwood (now First Wireless Operator), facing forward, with his buzzer on a ledge in front of him, and the big Marconi transmitter and receiver sets above. At altitude, his was the warmest situation in the aircraft, because the heating system reached it first of all, and Elwood could be sitting in a muck-sweat while the gunner in the nose was complaining of the perils to brass monkeys' private parts.

Further back along the fuselage, past the main wing spar (which resisted transit by any but a practised gymnast), past a small escape-hatch in the roof – small but important, as the nearest to the dinghy when it popped out of the wing – and past the euphemistically-termed rest bed, was Sergeant Overton's position.

He sat, half inside and half outside the fuselage, in the ovoid, perspex cocoon of the turret which, like the one in front, deployed two Browning guns. He could not wear his parachute-pack in the turret, for there was insufficient room, but he was not alone in that: most of the crew were in the same position. They wore the Irving harnesses and kept the packs in nearby stowages, hoping that there would be time, in an emergency, to locate them and attach them to the spring-clips on their chest-straps. Only the first pilot, if he chose, could wear a parachute with pack attached, which fitted in his seat; he, as captain of the aircraft, should be the last to leave and so have less time than the others to hunt round for his pack. In fact, as statistics were to show in later years, successful jumps from Lancasters in trouble would be relatively rare. Having found your parachute, and reached an escape-hatch or a door, which could be difficult if the aeroplane were burning or in a screaming dive (and if it were not, why should you want to leave?), you had to take your chance, once you had jumped, of tangling with propellers, wings or rudders. Given luck, determination and suffcient altitude, you stood a chance; flying low-level, your parachute might just as well be in the locker-room at base.

Still further aft along the fuselage – as far as anyone could go – was Sergeant Hebdon's lonely post, more than a cricket pitch's length away from where his fellow-gunner manned the turret in the nose. From his entry at the main door on the starboard side, he turned left, stooping (for the fuselage was slightly tapered, front to rear), and employing the Elsan toilet as a step – first making sure the lid was down – climbed across the tail-plane spar. Then he wriggled, feet first, through the sliding doors into the four-gun turret, plugged his lead into the intercom, and settled down to flying backwards for however long it took.

Sixteen aircrews, then, were preparing for the mission, but it was known that only twelve would actually fly it, and that four would be reserves. Knowledge of that sort could cause a man to search his soul: 'I wouldn't mind a chance to prang the Tirpitz,' he might think, or 'I hope to Christ it isn't us, if it's a daylight on the Ruhr!'

At that time, although both Squadrons were taking off and landing from their practice flights within a few miles of each other, few of the fliers knew that they were destined for a mutual adventure. Top Secret Order No 143, in fact, had detailed only six Lancasters for Augsburg (not that the aircrew knew that either), but since the issue of the order someone had decided that twelve aircraft together stood a better chance.

It was not until the final practice, on April 14th, that some of the pieces of the jigsaw fitted into place. The crews were briefed for a cross-country flight, a long one: from base to Selsey Bill, back north to Lincoln, on to Falkirk, then to Inverness, south to Wainfleet and back home to base. After take-off, the formations were to rendezvous over Grantham, and to fly together at low level all the way. Inverness would be their target for a simulated bombing run, and they would drop some practice bombs on Wainfleet target in the Wash before dispersing to return to base. For those who sought a clue as to where the practice might be leading, a round trip of about 1260 miles seemed to offer one. More than one observer set his dividers at 600 miles to scale, stuck one point into Grantham on the chart and swung the other in an arc which passed from north to south through the Norwegian fiords, the Baltic ports, Berlin, Leipzig, Nürnberg, across the south of France and out into the Bay of Biscay. That covered such a multitude of targets that nobody was very much the wiser.

The Grantham rendezvous did not take place. 97's six were there, but 44's were not – an outbreak of technical malfunctions had kept them on the ground at Waddington. Nor did 97's sections stay together through the trip, as they were meant to, for Sherwood's section, in the lead, flew too close to Daventry for comfort. Rodley, who was still flying first reserve, saw the BBC's transmitter masts ahead and sheared away. Surprised that Sherwood and his people had not seen them, he decided and afterwards proclaimed (false modesty was not a Rodley trait) that his eyesight was superior to theirs. Ifould, in the nose of Penman's aircraft, had also seen the hazard, and advised a change of course. Penman pulled away a few degrees, taking his formation with him. Gradually, the sections' tracks diverged. Sherwood missed the masts by several feet, and they went their separate ways to Inverness.

For the pilot, flying formation at low level could be fun, or just another chore, or bits of both. It depended quite a lot on whether you were leading or formating, and on whether it was loose or tight formation. The leader had the thrill of seeing the landscape rushing by – one of the few times in an aircraft when there was a sense of speed – and the fun of doing something that was normally forbidden, but the onus was on him to pick his course with care, especially in close formation, because the wing-men had no eyes for anything but him. If Number Two flew through a haystack, and Number Three pollarded several trees, the fault was not with them but with the leader. In a 'gaggle', flying loose formation, everybody could relax a little more, but the leader always had to keep his changes smooth and gentle, of either altitude or course, because of the inertia of the aeroplanes beside him. And more than half an hour or so of flying a heavy aircraft really low ceased to be fun, and increasingly became a muscle-aching, eyeball-popping 'bind'.

From Daventry they flew low until they reached North Yorkshire, where they had to climb above the stratus cloud that blanketed the moors. Beyond Carlisle, the sky was clear, and they crossed the Southern Uplands at about 250 feet, rising and falling with the shape of the terrain, climbing with the fells and descending with the waters. They flew across the gleaming lochs of Perthshire, where only the formating pilots could not pause to marvel at the scene, and climbed again above the Grampian Highlands, while the white-capped Cairngorms shone, still higher, to the east. Then, hugging the sloping coastal hills, they swooped on Inverness to make their dummy bombing run. By the time they were passing Edinburgh on the homeward route, they had really begun to get the feel of flying formation. Penman was as low as he had ever flown before: Deverill and Mycock were as tightly in beside him as a pair of fighters in a pre-war air display.

Cattle in their path stampeded, and Penman did not like to make that happen. 'Just can't avoid them,' he muttered apologetically, keeping steady on his course. Sherwood's section bombed the target in the Wash a few minutes ahead of Penman's, and they both had perfect bombing runs. Flying together back to Woodhall Spa, they made sure of passing over Waddington, low above the hangers and dispersals, where the groundcrews laboured on the aircraft. In 44's flight offices, the aircrews kicked their heels and got the message – 'Now what price the 97th foot?'

Next day, while 44 flew their cross-country to Inverness, Sherwood and Penman travelled to High Wycombe. Swearing them to secrecy, the Intelligence Staff produced a cardboard model, built to scale, and told them what it was. 'The M.A.N. factory – that stands for Maschinenfabrik Augsburg-Nürnberg Aktiengesellschaft. In other words, they make engines. Diesel engines, you know, for submarines.'

'Nürnberg, did you say?'

'Augsburg, actually – South Bavaria.'

'Christ!'

'What was that, old boy?'

'Nothing. Carry on.'

A target map showed the factory in the northern part of Augsburg, lying within a fork made by two rivers, the Lech to the east and the Wertach to the west – which had their confluence two kilometres further north. A canal served the factory as did a network of roads and branch lines of the railway. Lastly the airmen were shown an artist's impression of the factory as they would see it, approaching at low level from the south. Their target, they were told, was just one building in the

sprawling complex of sheds and offices and yards –
Halle E2, the main engine assembly-shop. That was the
bottle-neck in the production process: knock that out
and all the rest would stop.

Still slightly stunned, they nodded. They had heard of
bottlenecks before. Hit Essen hard enough, and there
would be no steel for Hitler's weapons; knock out the
marshalling yards at Hamm, and Hitler's railway system
would collapse. And so on. Nevertheless, they nodded.
'Where are the gun positions, do you know?'

'You'll be told all that sort of thing at briefing, on
your Stations.'

'When will that be?'

'Tomorrow, probably. Well, if there are no more
questions . . .'

2
Briefing – 1100 hours

They heard it all again at briefing, both at Woodhall and at Waddington. They heard how U-boat manufacture was geared to the production of their Diesel engines – the engines that powered them on the surface and recharged their batteries; how the slipways of Bremen, Kiel and Hamburg would be crammed with useless hulls if those engines did not roll off the line; how the end of the line was the assembly-shed at M.A.N. That was the bottleneck: that was their target. Not every airman in the briefing rooms took all this in – some were still boggling at those long ribbons on the wall-map. 'Don't be overawed,' they heard at Waddington, 'by the distance of the target. The position of our convoys in the Atlantic is critical. The RAF must strike this blow to help our seamen, and your Lancasters are the only aircraft that can strike it – with a fighting chance.'

At Waddington, there had been an audible intake of breath – a quiet gasp *con tutti* – when the route was first revealed. At Woodhall Spa, some men had burst out laughing, and enjoyed the joke until they noticed the expression on their Wing Commander's face. At that, the briefing room became a very silent place. They had gathered it would be a distant target: the trip to Selsey

Bill and Inverness had been a clue to that, as had the whisper in the morning that all fuel tanks were being filled up to the brim, but very few had seriously thought they would be sent to fly across a thousand miles of hostile territory in daylight. That kind of realisation tended momentarily to numb the thinking process. If you were knocked down over the Low Countries, or the south of France, you had at least a chance of dodging capture – of finding an escape route through the underground, of maybe getting home. Even if you went down in the drink, there was the possibility an Air-Sea Rescue launch would come and fish you out. But in South Bavaria? Some chance!

Not that any of these thoughts were spoken: no-one protested, no-one complained. That was not the way that you behaved. You might, on the evidence, conclude that the outcome of the briefing could only be your death, and you might not, at the moment, feel inclined to die. The trouble was, you were a volunteer (you would not be there if you were not): nobody was pressed into aircrew. And if aircrew sometimes had to die – too bad. So had lots of other people. True, when you volunteered it had not been with the thought of dying in the forefront of your mind. You had actually signed on for . . . what? The aircrew badge? The rank? To make your parents proud of you? Perhaps you should have listened to the veterans who said, 'Never volunteer'. Their likely comment now would be: 'You shouldn't have joined if you can't take a joke'.

They had all been kept in camp the night before the briefing, not allowed to use the telephone and excluded from the bar. Taken all in all, it had not been the jolliest of evenings. One young pilot took advantage of the waiting hours to read again the letter which, two days before, he had written home and placed, unsealed, inside his locker. He was Sandford's second dickey – Pilot Officer Hurworth Anthony Paul Peall, known on 44 as 'Buster'. His home was in Rhodesia. 'My darling Mother,' he had written, 'I knew from the start that this was bound to happen in the end, and I have always thought that my only regret would be not saying thank you, and goodbye. It seems strange writing so, but I feel I must. I will not begin to thank you for everything because words cannot express it, and anyway it would take far too long. Like Dad I am not afraid to die but just don't want to. But "God's will be done" so instead of coming home to you I go and meet Dad. I have heard how brave you were when Dad left us so I have no fear now. It is rather strange I should mention those words about God's will as I remember so well when I last said them. It was just before I passed out when in the sea that time. I should have loved to see you all once again Tricia, Guy and little Anthony, but that's how it must be, I suppose. You are a wonderful four and I hope you stick together and see Hitler beaten. But for you people there would be nothing in life to live for. Dear "Fatty" I wonder if he really remembers me or if he has just heard you talk of me so often. Actually I think he does remember me – perhaps in the swimming bath. God, what a home-life I have had. Everything a man could wish for and I don't think I appreciated it to the full. You remember Mum how I used to say, "When I find a woman like you, I would marry her tomorrow", I now realise that if I had kept to that and if I had lived, I should never have been married . . .'

He sealed the envelope, and put it back inside his locker.

*　　　*　　　*

The ribbon showed a route from Selsey Bill over the Channel to a little place called Dives Sur Mer, a few miles west of Deauville. From there it ran east-south-east, passing south of Paris, to a turning point on the River Yonne at Sens, then due eastward through the Midi, over the high ground of the Vosges, across the German frontier and the Rhine, to touch the northern margin of Lake Constance. There, the route swung slightly north of east, as though it aimed at Munich, but twelve miles short, above another, smaller lake – the Ammersee – turned ninety degrees to port for the run-up to the target.

The return route was just one straight line, from Augsburg to the Sussex coast, but the crews were told to use their judgement about that. If the timing worked out as it should, their bombs would fall on target with the last light of the day; but if daylight still prevailed when they turned homeward, they should stay south of German airspace, maintaining their formation and flying the outbound route's reciprocal, until darkness came to cover their retreat.

They were shown the model, maps and sketches that Sherwood and Penman had seen at High Wycombe, and told the way to recognise that one assembly shed. The factory's defences would be light – that was the Intelligence assessment, and they could just about believe it might be true. Jerry, probably, would never think that anyone could be so suicidally inclined as to attack the place. The outbound route, the briefing officers continued, had been carefully selected to pass clear of fighter airfields and, as an added safety measure, diversionary raids by thirty Bostons on Cherbourg and the Pas de Calais area, and massive sweeps by both the Fighter Groups, would be so timed as to ensure that all the Messerschmitts along the coast – and they could only be a fraction of the German fighter strength, since so many were deployed on other fronts – would be running out of fuel and ammunition when the Lancasters flew by.

At that, they relaxed a little in their seats, one glancing at another with a nod, even a smile, some lighting cigarettes. Maybe this Augsburg thing was not quite so suicidal as it seemed; at least, they were going to have some back-up over there. Bomber Harris, after all, would not throw them, and half his strength of precious Lancasters, away. They knew he was a hard man, but surely not that hard. And had he not, himself, been AOC of 5 Group, early in the war? Was it not known, through all the other Groups, that he loved them still? It was now 11.10 am, and take-off was four hours away. The briefings continued, identical at both the airfields except in style and presentation. 'Stores are four one-thousand pound GP bombs,' they heard at Waddington, 'with eleven-second delays, so each section should have cleared the target by the time they detonate . . .'

The Signals Leader at Woodhall Spa addressed the Wireless Ops. 'Maintain listening watch on the Group operational frequency. No WT transmissions except in emergency – same with RT between aircraft until you reach the target. Keep the IFF switched off during the outbound route – normal procedure on return to base . . .'

The Squadron Commanders took over to conclude the briefings. '. . . and stay below five-hundred feet,' said Wing Commander Collier of 97, 'until you're south of Paris. That should bring you in under the RDF. From there, it's up to section leaders to stay as low as possible consistent with safety. The lower you are, the harder you'll make it for the fighters. The same applies on the bombing run . . .' (he pointed at the model) 'but don't fly into any chimneys. If for any reason you're unable to bomb the factory, Munich or Nürnberg are the secondary targets . . .'

The forecast weather sounded fine – no cloud, good visibility all the way with a slight haze on return, wind east-north-easterly at 15 to 25 mph – but the Intelligence brief included something ominous, a message they had never heard before. 'Anyone who is shot down over France should make for Bordeaux, and go to the Black Cat café. If you come back okay . . ' (they marked that 'if') '. . . forget you ever heard of it.' They knew the French Resistance ran escape routes into Spain, but no-one until then had ever named a place. The valediction – 'Good luck, chaps' – was, as usual, delivered. It often seemed inadequate to the officers who said it, and never more than then, but what else was there to say? 'Have a good trip' seemed idiotic, 'Go ahead and kill yourselves – see if I care' was over-flippant, and 'Wish I were coming with you' invited an impertinent response. The crews stood up, filed slowly out, narrowing their eyes against the sunlight, and made their way to lunch. For twelve of them, it was to be their last in wartime England – for thirty-seven more, the last meal of their lives.

In Flying Control at Waddington, the second shift came on at one pm. ACW1 Beck, RT Operator, trotted up the concrete steps and took her station at the radio transmitter in the Watch Office. Little Phyllis Beck – or

Pip, as she was known to everyone – had arrived at Waddington with two other girls (the first WAAF RT Operators to be posted to the base) in the previous September, and had loved every minute of those seven months. She was nineteen, she was pretty and, to the bomber crews, she was the voice of Waddington. When they called 'Jetty' out of the darkness, the chances were it would be Pip, listening for the callsign, who would let them know that Waddington was waiting. Hers was the voice that meant runway lights on, feet on the ground, hot cocoa and a cigarette, bed in the billet, and another day tomorrow.

This time it was different: a daylight operation, take-off fifteen-hundred hours, and no-one seemed to know what or where the target was. They were never supposed to know, but someone always did. This time, a mystery. They settled down to wait for the action to begin.

Simultaneously at Waddington and Woodhall, a Very cartridge fired from the Watchtower balcony, made a slow, bright arc across the signals square. On each airfield, the engines of eight Lancasters were started, one by one. The propellers turned, the Merlins coughed, cleared their throats, and broke into their chorus. In their lofty cabins, the pilots watched the oil and coolant gauges – waiting for the temperatures to rise enough for test-running the engines.

These were anxious moments for four crews – those of the reserves on both the Squadrons. If all the first teams' Merlins sang in tune, if switching each magneto off in turn induced no serious decline in engine revolutions, if all the aircraft systems – hydraulic, pneumatic, electric and mechanical – seemed to function properly, the second reserves would shut their engines down and watch the others go; the first reserves would fly with the formations to the Sussex coast, in case a snag developed in the air, and then return. But, if any system or magneto failed, the first reserve would take the route for Augsburg in formation, and the second would turn back at Selsey Bill.

All the sights and sounds at Waddington were good: seven bombers lumbered from dispersal and the eighth shut down. At Woodhall Spa, Warrant Officer Harrison, No 2 in Sherwood's section, had an ailing engine. Despondently, he cut the switches: each propeller's whirling blur became distinguishable blades, which swung slowly to a halt. Rodley and his crew had seen the tell-tale puffs of oily smoke from that port engine, and had known just what they meant. It was no surprise to Rodley: that hollow feeling in his stomach as he walked towards the briefing-room had told him this was not to be one more cross-country – and that he was sure to fly. His anxiety had not seemed to centre on himself, but on his mother, and his wife – whom he had kissed as usual that morning, when he left their rented home in Woodhall Spa. For their sake he had determined to do all he could to bring himself, his crew, and F-Freddie home. One thing had troubled him: the only armour in the aircraft was behind his seat, not underneath, and it seemed quite possible that someone would be shooting at F-Freddie from that angle before the day was done. He had hurried to the armoury straight after briefing, but the Corporal had smiled and shaken an apologetic head. 'You're too late, Sir. We've had quite a demand for armour-plate today . . .'

The ability to improvise, so important to an officer in

wartime, had come to Rodley's aid. He had extricated the steel helmet from the bottom of his locker, and wedged it into F-Freddie's seat. It might not be the most comfortable of cushions, but it made him feel less vulnerable where it seemed to matter most. Seeing F-Freddie move, Warrant Officer Rowland took his place as flying reserve, and taxied out behind the other six. John Sherwood, leading the procession, brought K-King gently to a halt, still on the taxi-track beside the runway caravan. He looked at the brakes and set the throttle-levers for a steady, idling speed on all four engines.

Some pilots liked to have the second dickey read out the take-off check-list, pausing between items and confirming each was done. At night, this had the disadvantage that he had to use a torch, which was likely to impair night vision for a while, but it was a sure, safe method, and essential with an unfamiliar aircraft. Other pilots used a mnemonic they had learned at FTS (and so never would forget), such as T-M-P-F-F-G-G-H – for Trim, Mixture, Pitch, Fuel, Flaps, Gills, Gyro and Harness – and adapted it to suit the Lancaster. This was Sherwood's method and, aided by his second pilot, Webb, he used it now, with even more than customary care.

First, he moved the knobs below the throttle-quadrant to set the trim-tabs on the wings and tail: ailerons and rudders neutral, elevators two notches nose-heavy (that would help him get the tail up early on the runway and let the airflow give the rudders some effect).

'Throttle friction finger-tight,' he said, and turned the nut enough to stop the levers slipping backward if he took his hand away. Webb would clamp them fully forward when he called for take-off power.

46

'Superchargers – M gear.'

'M gear,' echoed Webb, and touched the lever that controlled the two-stage blowers – M for moderate at lower altitudes and F for full at height.

'Pitot heater – leave it off for now . . .' The airspeed indicator worked by measuring the airflow on the pitot-head, and the heater was supposed to stop it getting blocked by ice, in cloud or at height. Sherwood made a mental note to have Webb turn it on when they had bombed and turned (he crossed his fingers at the thought) to climb for home.

'Pitch – fully fine.' He slapped the propeller-speed levers with the flat of his hand. Webb screwed the friction-nut tight. 'And locked.'

'Fuel – contents?'

'All tanks reading full,' said Webb.

'Master cocks – on. Cross-feed cock?'

'Is off.'

'Booster pumps?'

Webb turned down four switches on the starboard cabin wall. 'Are on.' Sherwood moved a lever between his seat and Webb's, and watched one of the gauges on the panel. 'Flaps – fifteen degrees,' he said, 'and reading. Radiator shutters?'

'Switches on automatic.'

'Carburettor air-intake – cold. George . . .' (he tapped the automatic pilot controls on his side of the cabin) '. . . clutch in, cock out.'

He adjusted the cross-wires of the magnetic P4 compass, took the reading, and set it on the dial of the gyroscopic compass. 'Gyro set. Hatches?'

'Are shut.'

'Harness . . .' He felt the clasp of the Sutton safety-harness on his chest, and Webb tugged at his own lap-strap. '. . . is secure. Checks complete.'

He glanced through the open cabin window on his left. From the caravan, the Aerodrome Control Pilot was looking at him through the eye-piece of an Aldis lamp. Sherwood raised a thumb: the lamp shone green.

For a successful take-off in a laden Lancaster you needed steady concentration, a little strength in hands and feet, and some degree of skill – nothing superhuman – thousands of quite ordinary pilots managed it, time after time, in the ensuing years. There were, however, many who did not, and one reason for their failure was the tendency to swing which, with the Merlin engine, would always be to port, because the airscrews spun that way and their slipstream pushed that side of the fuselage, because of engine torque which made the aircraft try to turn round the propeller-shaft, and because of the attempt that any spinning axis makes, when pressed, to turn in its direction of rotation. You had to be prepared for swing on take-off, and not to let it happen. If it did, and you were late with your correction, you could get into another swing, this time to starboard, then back to port, and so on till the under-carriage broke or you ran out of airfield, or both. And aircraft full of fuel and high explosive ought not to be scraped along the ground.

Sherwood, knowing all this, set his right thumb well forward on the nearest of the throttle levers as he slowly pushed them open and set K-King in motion, very straight along the runway centre-line.

The needle of the ASI inched round the dial, and Sherwood's left hand, pushing forward on the wheel, turned the elevators down into the slipstream and what

48

little wind there was. Reluctantly, it seemed, the heavy tail-plane lifted, giving Sherwood the control of rudders that he needed, and giving Flight Sergeant Wilding, in the rear, relief from the bouncing and the shaking of his turret and the rumble of the tail-wheel underneath his seat.

Sherwood, with all the throttles at the gate and locked, had both hands free for the controls. Beside him, Webb was watching gauges, and would warn him instantly of any oil pressure drop or temperature rise, although there would be little he could do about that now. The crescendo of the Merlins filled his ears, the land beyond the runway's end was showing the shape of every hedge and tree. He was committed to the take-off. He did not really need to check the ASI for speed: the aeroplane was telling him itself, through every finger, just how close it was to flight. He checked it anyway.

At 105 mph, fifty seconds after the take-off run began, Sherwood's hands, with some assistance from 5,000 horse-power and the cambered upper surface of the enormous wings, lifted K-King's thirty tons into the air.

The front gunner, Sergeant Cox, had stationed himself beside the wireless operator during take-off (that was the safety order – no-one forward of the cabin until the Lancaster was airborne) and, through the perspex of the astrodome, had watched the airfield rushing past. Now he made his way towards the turret in the nose, edging past observer Hepburn's bench and crawling underneath the second pilot's seat. Arthur Cox was twenty-two years old, from Somerton in Somerset where, with his younger brother John, he had followed in a family tradition of devout adherence to the Christian faith – Sunday School, choirboy – at St Michael & All Angels' Church. If, three years ago, you had told young Arthur that, in the spring of 1942, he would fly to bomb a factory in Germany, his response would probably have been a polite but unbelieving smile.

The bombers took off singly and the section leaders kept their airspeed down until the wing-men had joined up. Again, the Grantham rendezvous did not take place. If it had, and 97's six had followed Nettleton, there might have been a different ending – a yet more bloody ending – to the story of the raid. But that was only one of many 'ifs' that would crop up, when there was talk and thought of Augsburg, in the days to come. As for Grantham, the failure of the rendezvous was no cause for concern among the pilots, nor even for surprise. They knew how difficult it was to find another aircraft in a given piece of sky. To find another seven should not, on the face of it, have been so difficult, but formations of big aircraft made wide turns – they could not circle, like a single aircraft, on a point. And it caused no great concern because they had never really thought about the raid as being essentially combined. The way each Squadron saw it, they were going to Augsburg – it just so happened that those other chaps were going there as well.

So they went their separate southward ways, 250 feet above the countryside – Nettleton with 44 and Sherwood leading 97. The sun was some way past its zenith (Double British Summer Time put two hours on to GMT), and had warmed the land enough to make the air peculiarly rough down at the bombers' altitude. To fly a tight formation was impracticable – bouncing and lurching in the turbulence, they kept their stations at a prudent distance. Over Selsey Bill, the seventh aircraft of each Squadron broke away. Mixed feelings of frustration, disappointment and relief passed through the minds of fourteen men – the feelings of the understudy not required to act, of the eleven's twelfth man never called on to the field, and of the patient at the dentist's whose appointment is postponed. This was not to be their day for action, not their day to do nor yet to die. They flew north in the sunlight to a silent, waiting base. The time was 4.15 pm.

Still separate, as they would remain throughout the mission, the formations set course south across the Channel – above that same expanse of moving water which, in deep and silent darkness, hid the bones of Rudolf Diesel, while his engines drove the vehicles of war. Twelve Lancasters were now committed to the raid. They are named below – the crews in order of the first and second pilots (the first being also captain of the aircraft), the observer, wireless-operator and three gunners – front, mid-upper (doubling as second wireless-operator) and rear.

44 Squadron (code letters KM, callsign 'Maypole'):

In R5508 B-Baker, Squadron Leader Nettleton (Rhodesia), Pilot Officer Dorehill (Rhodesia), Pilot Officer Sands (Australia), Sergeant Churchill (South Africa), Sergeant Huntly (Rhodesia), Flight Sergeant Mutter, and Flight Sergeant Harrison. And as formation leader, Nettleton had an extra man – Flight Lieutenant McClure (Rhodesia) – to read the map and aim the bombs, leaving Desmond Sands to concentrate on navigation.

In R5510 A-Apple, Flying Officer Garwell DFM, Sergeant Dando (Rhodesia), Flight Sergeant Kirke DFM

(New Zealand), Flight Sergeant Flux DFM, Sergeant Watson, Sergeant Edwards, and Flight Sergeant McAlpine (Canada).

In L7536 H-Howe, Sergeant Rhodes, Sergeant Baxter (New Zealand), Sergeant Daly, Sergeant Merricks, Sergeant Wynton, Flight Sergeant Edwards, and Flight Sergeant Gill.

44 Squadron's 2nd section:

In R5506 P-Peter, Flight Lieutenant Sandford, Pilot Officer Peall (Rhodesia), Flying Officer Gerrie, Sergeant Hadgraft, Sergeant Venter (Rhodesia), Sergeant Law, and Sergeant Wing.

In L7548 T-Tommy, Warrant Officer Crum DFM, Sergeant Dedman (Rhodesia), Sergeant Birkett, Flight Sergeant Saunderson, Sergeant Dowty, Sergeant Miller, and Sergeant Cobb.

In L7565 V-Victor, Warrant Officer Beckett DFM, Sergeant Moss (Rhodesia), Flight Sergeant Ross (Canada), Sergeant Seagoe, Sergeant Hackett, Sergeant Harrison, and Sergeant Trustram.

97 Squadron (code letters OF, callsign 'Lifebuoy', leading section:

In L7573 K-King, Squadron Leader Sherwood DFC & bar. Pilot Officer Webb, Flying Officer Hepburn, Sergeant Page, Sergeant Cox, Flight Sergeant Harrington, and Flight Sergeant Wilding.

In R5537 B-Baker, Flight Lieutenant Hallows, Pilot Officer Friend, Pilot Officer Cutting, Flight Sergeant Louch, Sergeant Jones, Sergeant Broomfield, and Sergeant Goacher.

In R5488 F-Freddie, Flying Officer Rodley, Pilot

Officer Colquhoun, Sergeant Henley, Sergeant Merrals, Sergeant Cummings, Sergeant Ratcliffe, and Sergeant Crisp.

97 Squadron's 2nd section:

In R5496 U-Uncle, Flight Lieutenant Penman DFC, Pilot Officer Hooey (USA), Pilot Officer Ifould (Australia), Flight Sergeant Elwood, Sergeant Tales, Sergeant Overton, and Sergeant Hebdon.

In L7575 Y-Yorker, Flying Officer Deverill DFM, Sergeant Cooper, Pilot Officer Butler, Sergeant Irons, Sergeant Mackay, Sergeant Devine, and Flight Sergeant Keane.

In R5513 P-Peter, Warrant Officer Mycock DFC, Sergeant Hayes, Warrant Officer Harrison, Sergeant Eades, Sergeant Macdonald, Sergeant Shelly, and Sergeant Donoghue.

These were the airmen who approached the coast of Normandy, flying very low across the water on that fine, clear afternoon. The air above the sea had lost its turbulence; the pilots' work was less exhausting, and the crewmen ceased to bounce upon their seats. The water, too, was calm – the slipstream of the aircraft stirred it as they passed.

It was at this time that Nettleton, checking the position of his wing-men, noticed that on both his own mainplanes, a shallow groove about two inches wide ran from front to rear. It occurred to him that possibly the turbulence above the land had caused some flexing of the spars. He put the matter out of mind, and turned his thoughts and eyes to France.

According to High Wycombe's plan, the diversionary 'circus' should have been beginning its performance at just about that time – 'Z minus 10 minutes', Sam Elworthy had written, 'Z being the time at which the bombers cross the coast', and it was clear that he had meant the coast of France. Either the plan had changed somewhere along the line, or everyone had got the timing wrong.

At one minute past 4 pm, twelve escorted Bostons had dropped four 500-pounders each from 12,000 feet on ships in the dry docks at Cherbourg. The rear 'vic' of three had been attacked by eighteen Bf 109s above the target. One Boston had gone down with both engines on fire. The Spitfire escort had claimed three of the Messerschmitts destroyed.

Eleven minutes later, another twelve Bostons had attacked targets further east from 10,000 feet. Half this force had bombed the Grand Quevilly power station, with moderate success, while the other six had bombed the shipyard at Rouen, scoring hits on ships at the jetties and in slipways, and on fuel tanks in the yard. Intercepted signals traffic indicated that between thirty-five and forty enemy fighters had been scrambled and directed to Rouen. The Spitfire pilots had seen fifteen of these, and dissuaded them from bothering the Bostons. Light flak had put up some opposition at the shipyard.

Throughout the fifteen minutes of the Boston attacks, the sky above the Strait of Dover had been thick with seventy-two more of 11 Group's Spitfires, and this had been exactly in accordance with their orders: 'Z minus 50 minutes', Flighter Command Headquarters had specifically decreed, in Most Secret Operations Order of 13th April, and had added 'Accurate timing is essential to the success of the operation . . .'

At 4.45 pm. thirty minutes after the last of the

Bostons and the last of the Spitfires had gone home, Nettleton's formation lifting just above the cliff-tops, crossed the coast and altered course south-east. It was then that Sherwood thought he saw them, for the first and only time, tiny in the distance on his left. Neither Hallows nor Rodley, concentrating on the leader, caught a sight of them: nor did any of the pilots in the second section, following some half a mile astern. Sherwood held a brief discussion with his navigator, Hepburn, who was known on 97 as a 'gen man'. Hepburn told him he was where he ought to be, and that was good enough for Sherwood. If those specks to port were Nettleton's formation, then it was they who were off course.

Further east along the coast, at a light flak battery HQ in Dieppe, Unteroffizier Albert Fackler heard of the bombers' coming from the radar unit co-located with his guns. 'Twelve aircraft, Corporal,' the Freya operator told him, 'about a hundred kilometres south-west.'

'Are they coming our way?'

'No, they're heading south-east.'

'Can you keep a check on them,' asked Fackler, 'and let me know where they go?'

'I'll do that, Corporal.'

Albert Fackler, it so happened, was an Augsburger.

3
'109s at eleven o'clock high!'

That part of the French sky through which the bombers had to pass was defended by Jagdgeschwader 2, with Major Walter Oesau in command. The Major, plump and baby-faced but cold of eye, had flown and fought for Germany since the beginning of the war, and had claimed his hundredth victory in October '41. He was a hero of the Reich – an ace. Nor had his unit (known throughout the Luftwaffe as the 'Richthofen' Geschwader in memory of the ace of World War I) been unsuccessful in its task, for its bag of Allied aircraft stood at three short of a thousand. The second Gruppe of JG 2, under Hauptmann Hiene Greisert, and the Stab (or Staff) Flight, were equipped with Messer-schmitts – the Bf 109F – and based at Beaumont-le-Roger. That afternoon, some thirty aircraft had been scrambled in response to an alert but, by the time they reached Rouen at altitude, the RAF had gone. Well, if the Geschwaderkommodore were not to write that magic 'thousand' in the record book today, so be it. The RAF would surely come again, and JG 2 could wait. They turned back to the west, and descended in a steady, shallow dive towards their base.

One of the pilots, for reasons of his own, was in a

hurry to be down. He pushed the throttle of the Daimler-Benz wide open, broke away from his companions, and swooped on Beaumont-le-Roger like an eagle on its prey. Straight-in approach, wheels down, green lights, the grass strip lying ahead. Automatically, his eyes swept round the airfield circuit – it was clear. Then he saw them, a few kilometres north – three four-engined bombers flying low in loose formation, and perhaps 400 metres after them, another three, all of a type that he had never seen before. He might not have seen them at all – their camouflage was good against the background of the fields – but that sharp glance around the circuit had revealed their great, black silhouettes against the sky. Once more, he thrust the throttle open, pulled up the wheels, and pressed the transmit button of his radio. 'Achtung – Tommis!'

In Crum's aircraft, flying on Sandford's left, Dedman had been trying to check their progress on the map, and finding it extremely difficult. One French village looked much like another and, at 100 feet, any landmark went by rather fast. Not that it mattered all that much – so long as Nettleton was there in front, Sandford would follow him, and Crum would stick to Sandford – but it was best to be aware of where they were for, if Nettleton went down, and Sandford got the chop, they would have to navigate themselves to Augsburg.

Such few folk as they had seen had seemed to welcome them: men had waved, and women had snatched sheets or towels from washing-lines to flutter as they passed. Indeed, Normandy's reception had been friendlier than that of Scotland on their practice flights, when shepherds on the hillsides had shaken angry fists among their scattered flocks. But above the woodland near Lisieux they had been fired on by a light flak battery, hidden in the trees, and they judged that Beckett's aircraft had been hit, either in the tail guns or in the pipes that served them, because the turret, which had ceaselessly rotated as Sergeant Trustram searched the sky, showed no more movement, and the Browning guns lay aimless in their mountings. The sudden smoke and sparkle of the flak had been a sharp reminder to the whole formation that this flight was no practice operation: a graph depicting the degree of their alertness would have, at that point, shown a peak.

It was Beckett who was first to see the fighters, slightly to their left and well above them – fighters that looked very much like Spitfires but were not, that were in fact the Staffeln of the 'Richthofen' Geschwader flying home to base. 'No RT transmissions, except in emergency' had stayed in Beckett's mind from briefing, but if this was not emergency he did not know what was. He pressed the transmit button: '109s at eleven o'clock high!'

Briefly Nettleton acknowledged, and told the wingmen to move closer. Rhodes and Garwell touched the throttles, nudged the rudders and the wheel. Four hundred yards astern, Crum and Beckett closed on Sandford. Fingers crossed, they told themselves that, with their upper surface camouflage, they might slip by unseen. Then Dedman saw the singleton, hurrying to land at Beaumont-le-Roger, and watched it closely, every sense alert. He remembered from the briefing that their route was meant to miss the fighter airfields, and wondered, for a moment, what the devil had gone wrong. Then he saw the fighter's wheels fold up into the wings, saw it moving faster as it swept across the field, and saw the Maltese Cross black-painted on the fuselage, the swastika on the fin. The long, grey nose swung round towards him. He tapped Crum on the shoulder and pointed at the fighter. Crum leaned across: the Messerschmitt was flying parallel, and climbing. Crum knew the fight was on. He settled in his seat, and made himself relax the tenseness of his hands upon the wheel.

The Messerschmitt's wings tilted as it turned for the attack. Dedman saw the flashes as the pilot fired his guns – two 7.92 mm machine-guns mounted on the cowling, synchronised with the propeller, and a 20 mm cannon in the hub. A bullet hit T-Tommy's 'glasshouse', and perspex splinters flew about the cabin. Blood trickled down Crum's cheek, falling on his harness strap, but the pilot answered Dedman's query with a reassuring grin. Crum had flown on many missions and been shot at many times: they had not hurt him seriously yet. For his gunners, on the other hand, it was their first experience of combat. They had fired at target drogues in training, but never at another aircraft, not at other airmen, and when fighters had flashed by them in the dark, on operations, there had really been no point in opening fire. But now they had to, if they were to stay alive. Now they had to estimate the range and the deflection, bring their guns to bear and squeeze the triggers. They had to try to shoot that Jerry down before he chopped T-Tommy.

But no sooner had the first rounds left the barrels of their guns, than the lone attacker had been joined by all the rest. Nettleton and Sandford, their wing-men close beside them, hugged the ground, leaving rippling wakes of flattened grass behind. At least they would present no easy target – no soft underbelly – to the swooping fighter pilots. Hauptmann Greisert, in the lead, selected Beckett's aircraft as his target, and he chose well, for Beckett had lost four guns out of six that could fire back. Greisert knew his cannon-shells had struck: a spurt of flame came from an engine and developed, feeding on itself, lighting fuel-tanks and fabric, playing along the fuselage until the aircraft was a torch. Greisert watched his victim fall astern of the formation, slowly losing height until there was no more to lose. V-Victor ploughed a blackened furrow through a field, smashed into a clump of trees, and thirty tons of steel and aluminium, wood and fabric, fuel-oil and rubber, of ammunition and explosives – all that and seven men – disintegrated into elemental debris.

All Crum knew of Beckett's end was what he could distinguish from his gunners' commentary on intercom through the background roar of slipstream and the rattle of the guns. He had eyes for nothing but his leader's aeroplane, though he knew well enough T-Tommy would be next for JG 2's attention. He also knew his duty was to fly his aircraft just as well, and for as long, as he was able.

Until the fighting started, the cabin had been warm, there in the sunshine, and he had been tempted to let Dedman hold the wheel while he took off his tunic; he was glad that he had not, for now there was a cold draught at his back. He did not know it, but behind him T-Tommy's fuselage was being ripped to shreds and tatters by Feldwebel Bossenkert of Staffel 5.

Someone said 'I'm hit,' and then again 'I'm hit!' it was fortunate for little Johnny Miller, manning the mid-upper turret, that the cannon-shell had merely put another parting in his hair. It was even luckier for Dowty, who stood six feet in his socks, that he had swopped with Miller for the trip.

The port wing trailed a plume of flame. With his left hand, Crum pushed the bomb-door lever down. 'Jettison the bomb-load,' he said into his microphone, but he could not hear his own voice through the headphones, and realised that the intercom had gone. He let the mouthpiece fall aside. 'Jettison the bombs,' he shouted, 'Jettison them on "Safe".'

Dedman pressed the button, and T-Tommy jolted as the thousand-pounders fell, unarmed, into a field. Like a boat half-full of water, the sinking aircraft wallowed on. Bert Dowty, in the front gun turret, watched the ground grow large ahead of him, until he could see each separate tuft of grass. 'My God, we're going to crash,' he thought. 'Crummy's going to fly us straight into the deck!' Instinctively, he tried to draw his knees above his abdomen: whatever T-Tommy was about to hit, he knew that he was pretty sure to feel it first. But Crum was in control, and – luckily for Dowty and the crew – he knew exactly what to do. He held T-Tommy just above the stall until the way ahead was clear of trees and poles and animals, and then he let it down – as gently and as carefully as anyone would ever land a bomber on its belly.

They scrambled out into the field – all, that is, except for Dowty. Try as he might (and he tried hard, because he was persuaded, not only that the aircraft was on fire, but that the bombs were still on board), he could not break his way out of the nose. He took the left-hand Browning from its mounting, and swung the muzzle hard against the perspex, but could not gain enough momentum in the space at his disposal. Then came Crum, who had stepped out of the cabin as a man might leave a bus, to hack an opening in the turret with a crash-axe. As Dowty crawled out, panting, Crum dropped the axe and looked towards the west, where a column of black smoke marked Beckett's pyre. He turned back to his crew. 'You know the drill,' he said. 'Destroy the kite and clear off. I want to see what's happened over there.'

They watched him set off, running, and felt no surprise: they knew that Beckett was his closest friend. Bomber men were careful about friendships on the Squadron – an unwritten code of conduct was observed. Crews stuck together, for the most part, although it was accepted there was nothing wrong with a relationship between men of the same category – say, between a WOP/AG of one crew and one of another – or who came from the same neighbourhood or had been to the same school, so long as such extraneous liaisons did not jeopardise the cohesion of the crew. But friendship between, as an example, the observer of crew A and the pilot of crew B would be regarded as unnatural, and in conflict with the code. Crum's fellowship with Beckett, based on shared experience and similar responsibilities, was acceptable to all. 'So long, Crummy,' Dedman called. 'See you back at Waddo!'

They turned away, staring at T-Tommy's hulk. The port wing's fire, starved of the stimulating slipstream, had gone out. For all its holes and shredded fabric the Lancaster – still on the secret list – was in one piece, as was the yet more secret 'Gee-box'. Birkett climbed in through the broken cabin-wall and pressed detonator switches to destroy the radar and the IFF. 'Bring the

Very pistol, Nicky', shouted Dedman, 'and some cartridges.'

A pair of fighters whistled overhead: the gunners named them as Focke-Wulfe 190s. Dedman, ignoring the diversion, fired a signal flare into T-Tommy's wing: no fire ensued. He fired another: still no fire. They attacked a wing tank with the axe and threw lighted matches on the stream of petrol (Dowty, quite illegally, carried cigarettes and matches in an old tobacco tin as part of his survival kit). At last the wing, the fuselage, and then the other wing burst into flames. They retreated, as the fire reached ammunition belts and rounds began to pop, and made their way into the shelter of the woods. They moved carefully, in pairs: Cobb with Miller, Dedman with Birkett (they had been together since the Hampden days – a powerful bond), Dowty with Saunderson. Bordeaux seemed a long, long way to go.

Already out of earshot to the east, the hunt continued, and Sandford in P-Peter was the target for the pack: Sandford, who always wore pyjamas underneath his flying kit, who had left his mongrel dog (inherited from a fellow-pilot) to wait for him as usual with the ground crew at dispersal, Sandford, who had called his mother, just before the use of telephones was banned, to expect him home next Tuesday, when his crew's turn for leave came up on the roster. He had been one of the first to fly the Lancaster, and had shown many more, from both the Squadrons, how to fly it, too. Now, he was to give a final demonstration of his skill. High-tension cables stretched ahead of him. lying straight across his course. With gritted teeth, and hands firm on the wheel, he flew beneath the cables. Three fighters followed, firing still. With all four engines burning, and a shattered fuselage, P-Peter smashed into the ground. It happened – as Buster Peall had known it would – and it happened very quickly, to them all. The Squadron Adjutant would cross the name of Sandford off the roster, and the next crew's leave would be advanced by seven days.

The final burst of cannon-shells which ended time for Sandford and his crew was fired by Unteroffizier Pohl, of Staffel 5. For him, it was a time of triumph: there would be celebrations at Beaumont-le-Roger, with cake and wine – perhaps champagne – and a party to remember, for the 'Richthofen's' one thousandth Tommi: and he, young Pohl, would the the hero of the hour.

Nettleton, with Rhodes still on his starboard wing and Garwell on his port, now knew from what his gunners said that half his force was gone. Harrison could offer no resistance from the tail – his guns were jammed – but Mutter, the mid-upper, was hitting back whenever an attacker was in range. The trouble was the pilots of the Messerschmitts need never come so near: with their more potent armament, they could open fire at 700 yards and close, still firing, to 400 and then break away. They knew well enough, if this new British bomber had machine-guns like the others, that any shot which reached them there was spent.

Major Oesau had no need to break away. His target was H-Howe and, on that aircraft, every gun was jammed. As Rhodes's gunners strove to clear them, Oesau closed until there was a cricket pitch's length between the Lancaster's rear turret and his propeller hub. He opened fire with the machine-guns and, using all his long experience, swung the nose from left to right to put a burst into each engine.

Squadron Leader John Nettleton VC who led 44 Squadron's Lancasters on the Augsburg
raid. He was the sole survivor from his formation of six. The citation to his Victoria Cross,
awarded after the Augsburg raid, referred to his qualities of 'skilled airmanship, leadership,
courage and determination'. He was later promoted to Wing Commander and became
Commanding Officer of 44 Squadron. On the night of 12/13 July 1943 he took off for a raid
on Turin but did not return.

Some of the 97 Squadron crews who returned safely from Augsburg:

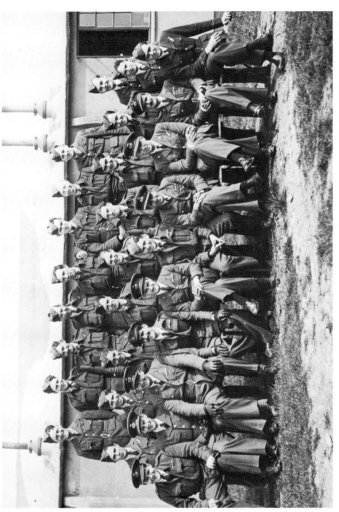

Back row (left to right):
Sergeant T. Goacher, DFM
Sergeant Merralls
Sergeant Crisp
Sergeant J. T. Ratcliffe, DFM
Sergeant D. L. Overton, DFM
Flight Sergeant Ellwood
Sergeant R. P. Irons, DFM
Sergeant Hebdon

Centre:
Sergeant Henley
Sergeant Cummings
Sergeant Jones
Sergeant Broomfield
Sergeant Devine
Sergeant K. O. Mackay, DFM
Sergeant Cooper
Flight Sergeant Keane
Flight Sergeant B. G. Louch, DFM
Sergeant Tales

Front row:
Pilot Officer Colquhoun
Pilot Officer Cutting
Pilot Officer Friend
Flight Lieutenant B. R. W. Hallowes, RAFVR, DFC
Flying Officer E. E. Rodley, RAFVR, DFC
Flight Lieutenant D. J. Penman, DSO, DFC
Flying Officer E. A. Deverill, DFC, DFM
Pilot Officer Butler
Pilot Officer G. C. Hobey, RAFVR, DFC
Pilot Officer E. W. Ifould, DFC

(Ranks and decorations as at the time of the raid)

Squadron Leader Nettleton's Crew

Back row, left to right:
Flight Sergeant L. H. Mutter, DFM;
Flight Sergeant F. H. Harrison, DFM;
Flight Lieutenant McLure, DFC;
Sergeant D. N. Huntly, DFM.

Front row, left to right:
Pilot Officer P. A. Dorehill, DFC;
Squadron Leader J. D. Nettleton, VC;
Pilot Officer D. O. Sands, DFC;
Sergeant C. F. Churchill, DFM.

Photograph: The Trustees of the Imperial War Museum

Lancaster B1, L7578, in which Nettleton and his crew practised briefly for the Augsburg raid.

Photograph: Hawker Siddeley Aviation Ltd.

UGSBURG.

Reconnaissance photograph (taken on 29 April 1942) of the bomb damage to the diesel engine factory at Augsburg.

Damage at Augsburg. One of the wrecked machine shops.

Photograph: M.A.N., Augsburg

Another direct hit at Augsburg

Photograph: M.A.N., Augsbu

One of the bombs that failed to explode.

Photograph: M.A.N., Augsburg

Wedding day photograph of Squadron
Leader John Nettleton and Section Officer
Betty Havelock – the Reception at the
White Hart Hotel, Lincoln.

Photo by Frisby (from the Garbett/Goulding collection)

A wedding day photograph of Warrant
Officer H. Crum and his bride. Warrant
Officer Crum, DFM AEM, who crash-
landed his crippled Lancaster successfully in
a field in France, became a P.O.W.

ACW1 'Pip' Beck (now Mrs Brimson of
Northampton) one of the RT operators on
duty at Waddington's Flying Control on the
day of the raid.

The death throes of H-Howe were terrible to see. At first, it put on speed, as though the throttles of the burning Merlins had been opened wide, and then it climbed, rearing like a frightened animal, and veered to port, until it hung directly over Nettleton and Garwell. They did not know if Rhodes was flying the aircraft or if it was flying itself, and that was never to be known, but whatever or whoever held the stick ran out of flying speed. Lift could fight with weight no more, nor thrust contend with drag. H-Howe hovered, stalled and fell, the nose descending like a headman's axe. In B-Baker and A-Apple, they flinched and held their breath. Some watched the flaming monster plunge towards them, others shut their eyes. To those who watched, it seemed to try to grasp them, as a drowning man might snatch at anything afloat. Then it was past, by inches, and struck the ground, and crumpled on itself, and disappeared in a kaleidoscope of flames and sparks and smoke.

Still the deadly chase continued eastward. B-Baker and A-Apple were repeatedly attacked, and trails of vapour from the wings revealed that fuel tanks were holed. But the trails decreased to puffs, and then to nothing, as the rubber self-sealing compound plugged the leaks. From B-Baker's astrodome, Charlie Churchill clearly saw the faces of the fighter pilots as they pulled away from their attacks. He noticed that the tip of Garwell's starboard mainplane, shredded by the bullets, flapped like a sparrow's wing. As the bombers swept across another village, both pilots saw the shots that missed them blowing gaps in walls and cottage roofs ahead. On Garwell's left, Underoffizier Edelmann, a Staff Flight pilot, came in from the beam, and kept on coming. (It is likely that his Oerlikon's magazine was empty – the Bf 109 could carry only 60 cannon-shells – and so he had to come in close enough to use his MG 17s.) As he broke away, he made himself a target for the front turret guns – two of the three that still would fire in A-Apple. 'This one's mine,' said Sergeant Watson, aimed, and squeezed the triggers. His aim was good: Edelmann, alone of the 'Richthofen' in that bitter combat, was hit by a .303 bullet. With some damage to the aircraft, he landed in a field (years later he would claim, with the well-developed sense of amour propre all fighter pilots shared, that the cause of his forced landing was an empty fuel tank.) In B-Baker, a splinter flew across the cabin. 'What the hell . . .' said Dorehill, and clapped a hand against his neck, as though a wasp had stung him. Nettleton glanced quickly at his second pilot's face, saw not hurt but indignation, and surprised himself by bursting into laughter as he turned back to his task. Then, suddenly, the sky was empty. JG 2, with both fuel and ammunition short, had given up the chase and disappeared as quickly as they came. The time was 5.15 pm. Of the forty-three young men who had set out from Waddington at 3 o'clock, twenty-one were dead and seven more were down, somewhere on the Plaine de St André.

4

'Fulmina Regis Iusta'

Nettleton and Garwell flew on to the east, still some
miles ahead and to the north of 97's aircraft. In
B-Baker, Pat Dorehill was conducting a private
reappraisal of the mission (which was his seventeenth).
He was a twenty-year-old Rhodesian, big and
handsome, with a cheerful attitude to life. Fellow-
members of the Mess at Waddington would long
remember him for an occasion at a party when,
standing – or rather gently swaying – with his back
towards an open window, glass in hand, he had tilted
just too far and disappeared, to be discovered later lying
in a flower-bed, with the smile still on his face and the
beer still in his glass. At the briefing he had not been
overly impressed, and not by any means downcast, by
the prospect of flying to South Bavaria in daylight. He
had quickly formed a high opinion of the Lancaster
and, in his view, the fire-power of the 44
formation – forty-eight machine-guns – would be
enough to deal with anything the Luftwaffe might pit
against them. He had been ready to admit that flak
might be a problem but, all in all, he had been looking
forward to the trip. JG 2's onslaught had given him
some cause to reconsider his opinion, and he rather

hoped that Desmond Sands would henceforth make a point of steering clear of fighter airfields. The crew had held a conference on intercom as to whether they should still go on with only two of the formation left, and had decided to a man that, since both the aircraft and the bombs were more or less intact, they should and must. (In this, they looked with Nelson's eye upon the order that, if any aircraft of a section fell, the section would turn back.)

Long before they crossed the Rhine, defence controllers in the south of Germany knew that the RAF were on their way and, judging by their course, that way might lead to Munich. The system of alarms was put in train: 'Air Danger 15', for civil defence and factories and hospitals, a quarter of an hour before the bombers would be near: nine minutes later, the 'Fliegeralarm' – two-second siren blasts repeated fifteen times – for the public to take shelter. The flak divisions of the Luftwaffe had a system of their own: on the first alert, passed by codeword 'Edelweiss', one man of each crew took station by the gun to act as look-out: on the second warning, 'Alpen Rose', the whole crew manned the gun. Meanwhile, the bombers spread their own kind of alarm – not among the public, for their route was sparsely populated – but among the cattle and the horses in the fields. The pilots saw a pair of riders fighting to control their rearing mounts, and the awful spectacle of Rhodes's final struggle with H-Howe came back to Garwell's mind.

Nettleton took B-Baker up a thousand feet or so to clear the foothills of the Vosges, and Dorehill's spirits lifted with the aircraft. He felt sure again that they would get to Augsburg. 'Okay if I go down the back,

JD,' he asked, 'and have a word with the rear gunner?'

He sidled back past Sands and Churchill (who was waiting at his set for the half-hourly broadcast from Group HQ in Grantham), climbed the main wing spar, passed through the armoured doors into the dark, rear section of the fuselage, walking on the floor above the bomb-bay, between the ammunition runways that led back to the guns. The sensations there were different from those up in the cabin – like walking down the carriage of a darkened subway train while it was making its best speed between the stations. He moved on, past Sergeant Mutter's turret, and gave the homing pigeons' box a friendly pat as he went by. There was a story, he remembered, of an observer, lost, who wrote prospective courses down and showed them to the pigeons until they indicated, by a nod, the one to get them home.

The little, oblong windows on each side of the fuselage gave just sufficient light for him to see the Lancaster's accoutrements around the entrance door: the master gyro-compass suspended in its cage (he noticed nothing wrong with it), the first-aid box, the ladder and the crash-axe in their stowages, and the dead-man's handle that would turn the turret fore-and-aft to facilitate the extrication of an incapacitated gunner. Flight Sergeant Harrison was by no means incapacitated, but his guns were – they had seized up after 40 seconds in the combat near Bernay. Like his fellow-gunner in the upper turret, he was a Cardiff man, and the Augsburg operation was his first (Mutter's experience was only slightly more extensive – he was flying his second). Both of them were hoping it would not always be like this. Harrison turned to smile at

Dorehill, pointed to the guns and, with a grimace, reverted to the problem of persuading them to work. In this, despite his every effort, he was not to be successful.

Dorehill, meanwhile, took the opportunity to use the Elsan toilet, before making his careful way back to the cabin. Once there, to complete his tour of all positions, he crawled into the nose alongside Charles McClure, who was peering through the flat bomb-aimer's window and matching the terrain against the map. Flight Lieutenant McClure was a South African, who had worked for Shell in Cape Town before he joined the RAFVR in 1940. He was the Squadron Bombing Leader and, of B-Baker's crew, the veteran, probably in terms of age – he was cagey about that – and certainly in terms of bomber missions, for Augsburg was to be his twenty-third. Beside him, on his right, he had the box of switches for selecting the stations in the bomb-bay of the bombs he had to drop and, ready to his hand, there lay the button he would press to make them fall.

'How's it going, Mac?' asked Dorehill.

McClure put his finger on the map. 'We're bang on track,' he said.

*   *   *

In old Augsburg, the sun was shining in the west, the weather fine and mild. The annual folk festival was in happy progress; bands were playing, people danced and sang in the mediaeval streets, sometimes in the shadow of the ancient buildings, sometimes in the brightness of the evening sun. Karl Dömling would like to have been with the 'Plärrer', but his duty called. Life for boys in Germany in 1942 was not a festival: if you were more than ten years old you had to be a Hitler Youth, and Karl, being all of twelve, was one of thirty boys who marched to the Haunstetter Woods, on the west bank of the Lech south of the town, for practice on the range.

Karl-Heinz Meinecke was seventeen, a type-setter at a printing works, living with his parents in the suburb of Kriegshaber on the west bank of the Wertach. He had learned to fly a glider, as did most of Germany's prospective pilots, had taken his 'C' licence – the highest category – and looked forward to the day when he would fly a Focke-Wulfe 190 or a Messerschmitt. He loved his flying, and the company of fellow glider-pilots. They talked together freely of the war and Hitler's Germany, no constraints, no inhibitions, not like his seniors in the town or work-mates at the printer's, whose words were always guarded and whose thoughts were seldom spoken.

Erika Harbacher lived with her parents in Oberhausen, another suburb on the west side of the Wertach, and to the north of Kriegshaber. Their apartment was in Tauscherstrasse, about 1,200 metres from the great M.A.N. engine works. Like Karl Dömling, Erika was twelve years old, but discipline for her was of a more domestic sort. Her duty, once her school work had been done, was to help her mother with the household chores. She was a cheerful, happy child and, while she worked, she liked to sing.

Johann Wagner's home was in Kriegshaber, as was Karl-Heinz Meinecke's, but nearer to the town, on the top floor of a block of flats between the Wertach and the railway line that ran to Nürnberg. At fourteen years of age, Johann was being trained for military service, as were his comtemporaries. In two years' time, he would be a Wehrmacht gunner, defending one of Germany's diminishing frontiers.

Lukas Kiermeyr, ten years older than Johann, was a medical orderly in the anti-aircraft arm of the Luftwaffe. He was currently attached to the crew of a 3.7 cm light flak gun. The gun was one of three that happened to be mounted on the roof of the assembly shed – 'Halle E2' – at M.A.N.

* * *

Apart from the strain of flying formation low – so low across the Channel that Rodley had remarked to his second dickey, the Canadian 'Junior' Colquhoun, that their airspeed should be registered in knots – the trip so far, for 97's six, had been uneventful. For David Penman, in U-Uncle, the only problem was with his rear gun-turret. Hebdon had test-fired the guns, once they were over water, and reported all in order. Then, half way to France he had discovered that the turret would not answer the controls. Penman considered this: he knew that, if the most Hebdon could do was turn the turret very slowly with the handle, he might as well forget about the guns for all the good that they would be in combat. However, Deverill and Mycock could give cover on both quarters and astern. He made his decision. 'We're not turning back now,' he told Hebdon. 'You'll have to do the best you can, and keep a good look-out.'

They crossed the coast unchallenged, flying without their jackets in the sun, and turned eastward, steady in formation at about 200 feet. Occasionally, people working in the fields stood erect and waved to them – one whipped his beret off and bowed a greying head. South of Bernay, on the way to Sens, two of the mid-upper gunners saw some sort of fracas to the north.

'Couple of kites going down in flames, skipper,' reported one. 'Can't tell what they are – too far away.' Nobody connected the event with Augsburg; no-one envisaged that those distant fires were burning men from Waddington.

From the turning point at Sens, they flew all the way to Constance without a sign of opposition from the air or from the ground, and with little sign of any sort of enemy activity. After they had crossed the Rhine, one solitary aeroplane – an Army Observation type – began to fly towards them, and then quickly turned away; a little later, Deverill, on Penman's left, caught sight of a soldier, who stared up at the Lancasters and ran into a building to report (decided Deverill) the direction of their flight. Sherwood's section passed above a railway station, and Hallows's gunners sprayed a waiting train with .303. Then a squad of soldiers, undergoing PT, broke ranks and ran for cover when another gunner – more in devilment than serious intent – fired a burst towards them. 'Look at the buggers go,' he commented. 'A credit to their PTI, they are.'

'Okay, cut the chatter out,' replied his pilot, 'and don't waste ammo.' It was not until they reached the northern margin of Lake Constance that anybody offered them resistance. There, a red-faced German officer, standing on the aft-deck of a white-painted ferry boat, pulled an automatic pistol from the holster on his hip and vainly fired a clipful at the bombers as they passed. Seeing this rather as a gesture than a threat, and respecting neutral waters, the gunners held their fire. Sherwood swung his section to the left, and Penman's section followed. They levelled out on course for the next turning-point, heading east-north-east.

The lake behind them shone like ancient silver; their shadows ran before them on the gently rising ground. The time was ten minutes past seven; the target lay a hundred miles ahead.

In Dieppe, the rader man reported back to Albert Fackler. 'They've been located over Constance, Corporal,' he said. 'We think they're making for Munich.'

Fackler considered this. Maybe the bombers' target was in Munich: but, just possibly . . . he picked up the telephone again. 'Get me an Augsburg number, please, operator. Military priority.'

'Lines to Augsburg are engaged, caller. I'll connect you as soon as I can.'

Nettleton and Garwell crossed the north edge of the Ammersee and swung to port, following the river that would lead them into Augsburg. They had twenty miles to go – six minutes' flying time.

The boys in the Haunstetter Woods, intent upon their training, took little notice of the sirens. It was not until they heard the rumble of the Merlins, far away as yet but growing louder, that they turned southward from their targets, one by one, and fell to silence, peering through the trees. The bombers thundered past them, flying above the river, very low. Karl Dömling saw the roundels on the fuselage and gasped with shock. He had not seen an enemy of Germany before.

The airmen in the bombers also faced a new experience: to come upon their target at low level in the daylight was altogether different from flying high at night. They would normally have known what lay ahead by now, they would have seen the flak, the searchlights, and the bright, white spurts as early bombs exploded on

74

the ground – all the stimuli required for stiffening their sinews and summoning the blood. This approach was blind, despite the daylight; what they might expect to see was only in the mind, a memory of the model and the artist's sketch.

The battery at M.A.N. had received the message 'Edelweiss', and a gunner from each crew in Halle E2 had hurried up the stairway to the flat roof of the shed. On the great tower of St Thaddeus, a thousand metres to the west, and on tall buildings elsewhere in the town, other watchers took their posts beside the 3.7 cm guns and 20 mm cannon. On Gablingen air base, nine kilometres west, the heavy guns were similarly manned. Then 'Alpen Rose' came through, together with the public warning, and with a supplementary order from divisional HQ: 'Fire only at clearly recognised enemy aircraft – you are warned that friendly aircraft are in the vicinity.' From this, the gun crews guessed that the flying school at Gablingen had u/t pilots in the air. Lukas Kiermeyr's corporal frowned: did Division think he couldn't tell a British bomber from a trainer? Anyway, it was probably all a false alarm; the Tommis could never fly so far across the Reich, certainly not in daylight. Nevertheless, he told the crews to load the guns, and kept an eye upon the western skyline.

There was no proper fighter force in southern Germany: the Jagdgeschwaders were deployed in western Europe, in the north and on the Russian front. The local fighter training schools, however, like Gablingen, had been alerted when the flak divisions were. A motley group of trainers had been hastily directed to patrol the environs of Munich at high altitude. Earnestly, and somewhat nervously, the

75

student pilots climbed hard to the east, while the Lancasters swept towards their target from the south.

That Augsburg was the jewel of Bavaria was no business of Nettleton or Garwell: that it was Europe's richest mediaeval town, spectacular with ramparts, towers and fountains, Gothic churches and Renaissance palaces, was not what brought them there. They had come because Doktor Rudolf Diesel, fifty years before, was given leave to build his engines there. That was their concern.

They eased the Lancasters up across the sloping woodland and saw the town ahead, long-shadowed in the slanting sun. John Nettleton had no time for the view: he was searching for the point where the canal forked north-west from the river to the factory. He found it in a second, saw the sprawling plant alongside the canal, and began to turn B-Baker's nose towards the target. Then he saw the chimney-stacks ahead: one aircraft might have passed between them, but not two. He rolled out of the turn, flew on past the chimneys, and chose a clear approach. It may be that the people of the Plärrer in the streets below had failed to hear the sirens through the festive noise or, having heard, elected to ignore them. However that may be, they pointed, laughed and waved as the Lancasters roared by. Then they heard the rapid banging of light flak and the rattle of machine-guns, and realised the truth. Suddenly, the festival was over.

One kilometre away, outside Halle E3 – the 'Hammer Schmiede' next to the assembly shed – the night-shift men, as careless of the warning as the thousands in the streets, had lingered in the yard to watch whatever fun there might be going on. It was only when the Lancasters appeared above the town, with bomb-doors gaping wide, and flying straight towards them through the flak, that they, too, realised what was happening, and that it was no fun at all.

The aircrews also heard the detonations, above the howling of the slipstream and the rumble of the Merlins, as the tracer hosed around them and the flak shells burst close by. In the combat near Bernay, most of the action had been with the top guns and the tail, but now the front guns had their chance. This Buzz Huntly in B-Baker and Jim Watson in A-Apple seized, with both hands on the triggers, and Huntly thrilled to see one gun-crew scatter from their post.

Before them lay the great sprawl of the factory. Somewhere among the shapes and shadows of those close-packed buildings lay their target, and it was coming nearer at 200 mph. McClure had the data in his mind – a two-storeyed shed, 300 yards long and 100 yards wide – that and his memory of the model and the map. He was entirely concentrated on the task of recognition; if guns were fired at him, he did not notice them. He saw the narrow, shining line of a canal, a footbridge over it, a rail-track curving in between the sheds and – there, that was it! That must be it! 'Bomb doors open,' said McClure, and gently set his thumb on the bomb-release button.

The closer B-Baker came to the shed, the less Nettleton could see of it-the aircraft's nose was in the way-but McClure had the target in his sights, and he was in control. Whatever course corrections he required, Nettleton would make at his command: 'Steady', 'Right', or 'Left' (always repeated – 'Left, left' – so that the sound would give the meaning even if the words did not come clearly through the pilot's headphones).

In A-Apple, Flight Sergeant Flux, the wireless-operator, was standing in the cabin, behind the pilots' seats. It was the post that he had taken up during the early combat, to make another pair of eyes to watch the fighters, and a voice to warn the pilot and the gunners of their threat. He knew well enough when he should speak, and when to hold his tongue, for he had been in combat many times. Now was a time to speak. 'We're on fire, Skipper,' said Bob Flux.

The ancient elements of earth, air, fire and water can all be terrible, when in disorder. Earthquake and hurricanes and floods are frightening enough, in the way they show a man his frailty, his tiny stature in the business of existence. But fire can bring the very worst of fears, and that may be why Hell, as we envisage it, is an inferno. The sight of fire, the smell of fire, where no fire ought to be, can obliterate the faculty of reasoning, erase the civilising centuries and, in their place, set panic. Not to yield to that instinctive fear has always needed fortitude. Garwell had his share of that and more.

One glance across his shoulder was enough: the fuselage, aft of the cabin, looked like an open furnace. He turned all his attention back to keeping station on B-Baker's wing, and his hands and feet were firm on the controls, although his thoughts were with the gunners in the back. Whether Edwards and McAlpine were already overcome, or were doing what they could to fight the fire, he had no way of knowing, but he knew that A-Apple was still answering his touch, and that he had a bombing run to make.

'Shut the fire-doors, Bob,' he ordered. 'Quick as you can.' Flux hurried aft, past the vacant navigation table

(Frank Kirke had been beside the bombsight since they left the Ammersee), and slammed the armoured doors that shut the cabin off from all that lay behind.

At four minutes to eight, the Lancasters of 44 came on their target like a double thunderclap. 'Bombs gone,' McClure told Nettleton; 'Bombs gone,' Kirke called to Garwell. Neither pilot needed the report, for they had sensed the very second when the thousand-pounders fell, from the way their aircraft seemed to leap at the release. Nettleton took his left hand off the wheel to pull the bomb-door lever closed, and smoothly swung B-Baker's nose to port. Garwell followed, not so smoothly, for the flames were feeding on A-Apple's vitals.

None of the gunners on the roof of Halle E2 had seen a Lancaster before, but there was neither time nor need to 'clearly recognise' the enemy, and all three guns had quickly opened fire. Lukas Kiermeyer, with a haversack of medicants and dressings on his shoulder, had stood and watched the bombers coming at him. For a moment it had seemed that he was living in a dream. He had said (or thought that he had said, for no voice could be heard) 'Dear Lord, protect us,' as he saw the thousand-pounders drop out of the bomb-bays. The bombers had roared overhead, one trailing smoke. Some instinct – some memory of his training – had told him that the casualties, if casualties there were, would be on the ground floor of the shed, and his duty was with them. He was half-way down the stairs when the first bomb detonated and, although the blast-wave threw him down to the next landing, the structure of the stair-well saved his skin. The next bomb fell into the gun-crew's living quarters, twenty metres from him, smashed through a wall, and did not detonate. Deafened, winded, Kiermeyr gave due thanks to God.

Nettleton had started counting from that second of release, and at 'ten' he turned to starboard, heading west, to bring the factory into vision on his right. On 'eleven', he saw the sudden flash and ripple of explosions, saw sections of the upper floor burst outward, and pieces of roof shoot high into the air. Then, as the scene became a blur of smoke and debris, he looked back to port, but Garwell was not there close in beside him, as he had been since they taxied out at Waddington, almost five hours before. Anxiously, he searched the sky. 'Can you see A-Apple, rear gunner?' he called.

'Starboard quarter, Skipper – a bit above us. I think he's got a fire in the fuselage.'

The switchboard operator in Dieppe had at last connected Fackler with his home.

'Mother,' he said, 'it's Albert . . .'

'Albert! Are you all right? Is anything wrong?'

'No, I'm fine, Mother. I'm ringing because . . .'

'I can't hear you very well, dear. There's an air raid going on.'

'Going on now? You should take shelter . . .'

'There, some more bombs. Can you hear them? It's a lovely day here, Albert, how is it with you? Are you sure there's nothing wrong, dear?'

In A-Apple, things were badly wrong: Ginger Garwell was fighting for his life, and for the lives of his remaining crew. In this fight, the odds were stacked against him, for the aircraft was not easy to control, and the country west of Augsburg was well-wooded, undulating, and criss-crossed by tree-lined lanes between the villages, with little space for making a forced landing. But the choking, blinding smoke which, seeping through the fire-doors, filled the cabin, was the greatest handicap of all. Bob Flux, a good man in an emergency, reached up and turned the handle in the roof – the escape hatch flew away. The slipstream, singing a crescendo in their ears. sucked smoke out of the cabin and, for a moment, they could breathe. Garwell saw a line of cottages ahead, an open field and, further on, a railway bridge across a road. Then the smoke was in his eyes and throat again, but he had seen enough.

A-Apple slid for fifty yards across the field. Half-way, it broke in two, aft of the wings, where the fire had eaten out its spine. Bruised and shaken, spluttering and coughing, Garwell clambered out, and with him Dando, Kirke and Watson. They found Flux's body, lying beneath the starboard wing. He must, they thought, have been flung through the escape hatch when A-Apple hit the ground, and carried by the aircraft to its final resting place. The means that he had used to aid his pilot's fight for life had also been the means of his own end. To his next-of-kin, Garwell was to write a letter two months later from a German prison camp: 'Throughout the raid he behaved splendidly . . .' From Garwell, such a judgement would be worth having.

B-Baker's gunners told their captain as much as they could see of what had happened to A-Apple, and Nettleton turned away south-west, striving to collect his shocked and scattered wits. This was no time to relax – he had to concentrate. The sky was still too light for him to take the straight route home through Germany and, for a moment, he was concerned at that, because according to the plan their departure from the target should have been at dusk. He put the thought aside: he would return the way he came, and climb when darkness fell. One Lancaster at least, he was determined, would fly back to Waddington.

5

97 Squadron on Target

As 44's B-Baker flew away from Augsburg towards the
setting sun, 97's leading section thundered up the valley
of the Lech in tight formation. Nettleton and Garwell,
by their direction of approach and perhaps because
some gun-crews could not immediately believe the raid
was really happening, had achieved, if only partially,
that precious element in air attack – surprise – just as
the planners at High Wycombe had intended that they
should, and they had flown so low that heavy guns had
not been brought to bear. Not that the light flak
batteries had failed: they had reacted well enough to
knock one bomber down. How they had cheered and
shouted when they saw that sudden gush of flame,
followed by the column of grey smoke that was rising
over Schlipsheim in the west! And they were really ready
now, for whatever was to come: a battery awaiting
redeployment in the railway loading bay had been
brought into action, and the barrels of the heavy guns
were down to full depression. All Augsburg's armament
was pointing at the skyline to the south.

They fired everything they had at Sherwood's section,
regardless of the damage they might cause to Augsburg's
walls and rooftops, but the enormous Tommi bombers

still came on, fast and low, straight at the factory. It was when their leader climbed to clear the chimneys – they must have been at least 100 metres up for several seconds – that was when the gun-crews should have got them, but, although it seemed impossible that anything could pass unscathed through all that shot and shell, the bombers still flew on. Some of their bombs fell through the roof of the assembly-shed, some on the access road close by.

The bombs fell with a whistle and a crash, but no explosion – not at once. The light flak hit the leader seconds later, just behind the inner engine on the left, and the gun-crew knew that they had struck a petrol tank, because the flames were sudden, bright and all-consuming. Still the little turret in the bomber's tail fired back – they could hear the bullets smack into the sandbags round their post – and it continued firing till the aircraft disappeared. Although they did not know it, they had scored another hit above the factory, with a shell that went clean through the starboard wing of Hallows's B-Baker, close to the fuselage. It did not seem to cause the structure serious damage, but the impact and the bang were just enough to put observer Cutting, at the bombsight, off his aim. He pressed the button fractionally late and realised, with chagrin, that his bombs would over-shoot.

Rodley's personal protection – the upside-down tin hat – had caused him some discomfort all the way: now he knew that it had been worth while. He had plunged down to 200 feet as soon as he had cleared the chimney stacks, and approached the target through a barrage of light flak which rattled on the fuselage like lead shot in a can. He also saw the big, black smudges of the heavy flak around him, and ruefully remembered that, according to the briefing, the 8.8s could not be brought to bear on aircraft flying low. His first impression of the assembly-shed was that it was just too narrow to be hit by all three Lancasters at their angle of approach: even if the leader hit the very centre, the wing-men's bombs would fall upon the walls on either side, and if the leader were the slightest bit off line, then No 2 or No 3 would miss the target altogether. He therefore fell a little back from Sherwood, and as close behind as he could fly without being buffeted by slipstream; then, at the second of release he swung the wings to give a sideways moment to the bombs' trajectory. (He was convinced that he had hit the target on the nose by this device, although Sergeant Henley's view was that the bombs fell on a building east of the assembly shed.) He saw white vapour trailing back from one of Sherwood's engines, and thought at first that it was coolant, but then the white turned black, and Rodley knew that petrol was on fire.

K-King, glowing like a blow-torch, slowly swung to starboard, until its course was practically due north. The 8.8 guns on Gablingen Airport opened fire, although there really was no need. 'Christ, Skipper, he's going in,' cried one of Rodley's gunners, 'A flaming chrysanthemum!'

Before the section's bombs exploded in a salvo of reverberating, eardrum-cracking noise, K-King had hit the ground. Everyone who saw that cataclysmic crash believed that all the crew were instantaneously dead. Yet Sherwood, still strapped into his seat, was thrown out of the cabin like a stone thrown from a sling; the branches broke his fall and he, alone of K-King's complement, survived.

84

Brian Hallows was, at twenty-six, by two years Rodley's junior in age and, as to operations, he had flown six to Rodley's eight; but, as a Flight Lieutenant, he was senior in rank, and it was he who took the lead position after Sherwood had gone down. Each was glad to have the other close for comfort and, in Hallows's case, for cover – Rodley still had guns that could be fired. 'The quintessence of loneliness,' mused Hallows, 'is being five hundred miles inside enemy territory with one serviceable turret.'

For an hour or more, they flew westward at about a thousand feet – 'not among the trees and bushes,' Hallows judged, 'but low enough' – then, when the sky was dark and they had almost reached the Ruhr, they climbed to a more comfortable altitude for the long ride home to Lincolnshire and base.

On that homeward flight, a pilot's thoughts could wander, undirected, along peculiar by-ways of the mind. One of these led to euphoria – a tendency to see the trip as virtually over. The nasty part was done, the target far behind, and all you had to do was to sit back, with a finger on the wheel (the aeroplane, without its load, was lovely to control) and let the world go by below. You could have been an airline pilot, flying a well-known route. It was a nice sensation; the trouble was, it led to sudden death. If you aspired to be, one day, an old bomber pilot, you had to recognise that feeling, and put it right out of your mind. You had to sit up straight, and remember where you were. Then came the antithesis: the sky around you slowly filled with menace, with unseen fighters homing in and sneaking up beneath your tail. You had to call the gunners, and make sure they were alert. Perhaps you ought to weave about a bit, as well. And those flashes in the distance, right ahead, two or three in quick succession – were they caused by trams? Electric trains? Or were you heading for the centre of a flak-belt? 'Pilot to observer, are you sure of our position?' The revs on the starboard outer seemed to fluctuate a lot. And was that really all the fuel you had left? Had the intercom packed up? You had better make a check round all the crew . . .

No-one could maintain that hyper-active, apprehensive state for long; it was a sure way to develop the condition called 'the twitch', symptoms of which were a noticeable difficulty in tying up your shoe-laces, or in drinking from a glass without using both hands.

What you had to do was try to keep your mind, and the aircraft, reasonably straight; not too relaxed, nor yet too tense. You had better try to think of something real, and sensible. Like the far horizon, or the clouds, or all those millions of stars. And you could listen to the rumble of the engines – there was nothing wrong with them – just the merest flicker on the starboard outer's gauge – their sound was deep and comforting, droning on for ever . . . and ever . . .

Suddenly, appalled, you were awake, and knew that you had slept – for a second, several minutes, for how long? Sweating, you would scan the dials, to see if anything had stopped, to check if you were still on course, and at the proper height. You would revile yourself: the crew relied on you to get them home, the least that you could do was stay awake. You would tell someone to find the thermos, slip your mask off for a moment, drink some coffee. Think of Mother, think of girls – they, too, would want you to get home.

Penman, with the second 97 section, having no desire

to be above the target when the time-delays on Sherwood's bombs expired, led Deverill and Mycock on two orbits of the Ammersee before he made his run. Then, heading in towards the factory, he saw the long, flat roof of the assembly-shed, with gaping holes made by the leading section's bombs, and the flicker of the flames that showed where fires were breaking out. He saw the tracer-bullets, too, glowing in the last light of the day, curving slowly up towards him – so slowly, as it seemed, that the impulse to evade was very strong. 'No weaving in formation,' Penman told himself, and held U-Uncle straight. 'Steady', chanted Ifould from the bombsight, as though to strengthen his resolve, 'target's coming up nicely . . . steady . . . steady . . .' At that moment, with three miles to run, Y-Yorker, on his left, was hit – a cannon-shell going through the starboard wing – and P-Peter, on the right, received a mortal blow. To those who watched, it seemed the shell hit Mycroft's aircraft in the forward turret, and they believed that it had two effects: the first, to kill or gravely wound MacDonald, the front gunner, and the second, to ignite the turret's oil supply – oil that pulsed throughout the aircraft like blood around the body of a man.

That was the moment some men would have chosen to give up the fight – wiser men, perhaps, than Mycock, or maybe lesser men. They would have jettisoned the bomb-load on whatever lay beneath, and put the aircraft on the ground before the fire took hold. Mycock did not adopt that course. He was slightly-built, with ginger hair, and he had won his DFC in circumstances almost as adverse. Now, as Garwell had (another ginger-headed pilot) and Sherwood, he stayed steady on the run until he knew the bombs had gone. Deverill's mid-upper gunner saw him, through the open cabin window, sitting upright at the wheel. Then P-Peter reared, swung to the left, passed over Penman's aircraft with its bomb doors still agape, and plunged into the ground.

Penman, meanwhile, saw a shell rip through the cowling of the inboard engine on his left, some six feet from his seat. 'They're bound to hit us,' he decided, 'the only thing that matters is whether they hit a vital part . . .' Above the factory, Deverill's Y-Yorker was hit again, and oil was set on fire in the pipes which served the upper turret and the rear; there Flight Sergeant Keane, finding that he could not move his guns, was moved to blasphemy: a moment earlier, with one well-directed burst, he had silenced a machine-gun on an office-building roof, and he was warming to his work.

Deverill's long experience of flying over water was not his only interest in the men who fought at sea, for his father was aboard the cruiser Ajax in the South Atlantic, when the battleship Graf Spee was hunted down. That Deverill, of the Senior Service, would have approved the way his son's crew worked in emergency: while Butler coolly aimed the bombs, Mackay and Irons between them fought the fire, and put it out.

Y-Yorker was still flying, but was not unscathed. The outboard engine on the left had stopped, and the turrets at the back had no hydraulic power, but Deverill, his duty done, now directed all his energies to bringing crew and aircraft home. Penman, having bombed, had put on speed and turned away at tree-top height. He did not see A-Apple's broken hulk, four miles westward of the factory, although he tasted smoke and knew that down there something burned; he did not see, and could not know, that Garwell, forlorn but full of pride, stood up and waved as he roared overhead. What he saw, with some surprise, was Deverill's Y-Yorker, with one propeller feathered, overtaking him, and as the only voices he had heard for many hours were those of his own crew, he was even more surprised when Deverill addressed him on RT. 'Hello, Lifebuoy U-Uncle, this is Y-Yorker. Are you receiving me? Over.'

Penman considered for a moment, and decided the approach was quite in order – RT silence could officially be broken now the target was behind them.

'Receiving you strength five,' he answered. 'Pass your message. Over.'

'My rear and mid-upper turrets are u/s. Can you give me cover, if I take the lead? Over.'

The Edinburgh man was never one to make decisions hastily, and did not do so now. He told Deverill 'Stand by', and consulted his observer, whose ability and judgment he held in high regard. Ifould had no doubt about the matter: 'Stay in the lead, Skipper,' he advised. 'I'll navigate us home.'

Penman also questioned Hebdon. 'Any joy with your guns yet, rear gunner?'

'Sorry, sir – no joy at all.'

That settled it. 'Lifebuoy Y-Yorker from U-Uncle, resume station. Over.'

That was how they flew back over Germany and Belgium, climbing to 18,000 feet when darkness came, with Deverill in close formation under Penman's wing. He had a try at starting the port outer on the way and, by some mechanical chance, the engine caught, and ran.

6

Aftermath in Augsburg

Back to the east, the makeshift fighter force had landed at the flying schools, The pilots had not seen a British bomber and, to a man, they blamed Defence Control: what deeds might they have done, had they been properly directed! Meanwhile, in the Haunstetter Woods, the boys were marching home, full of the excitement of the day. The impulse to talk about the raid was strong, but discipline was stronger, and they marched in silence. The time to talk would come, at home tonight and school tomorrow. For Karl Dömling, the image of the scene was set for ever in his mind: the thunderous passage up the river of the Lancasters, the shaking detonations, the towering palls of smoke. He had been fearful for his parents, living in the town, until he had seen the aircraft flying on, through the sparkle of the shells, and had realised that the town was not their target. By the time the rattle of the gunfire had reached him in the woods, the bombers, at a distance, had looked cumbersome and slow; one had seemed to vanish in a blinding flash of flame; another, sinking, trailed a long, black plume of smoke. He thought he had seen parachutes, and had been glad of that: the airmen might be enemies, but they were brave: as prisoners, they could fly against the Fatherland no more. (That there were parachutes, though not impossible, was most unlikely. If any airman used one, he did not survive. It was more probable that what Karl saw were flak-bursts.)

Erika Harbacher, watching with her father from a window of the Oberhausen flat, had seen the leading bombers, some obviously damaged, disappearing in the west. One, however, of the last formation, had flown low overhead, so close that she had clearly seen the British pilot, sitting upright at the wheel. Behind him, the aircraft was aflame. Erika would never know what made her run out of the garden and follow the long trail of smoke: perhaps it was excitement, appealing to the nature of a tomboy, twelve years old: perhaps it was the thought of that young airman in the cockpit.

Beside the railway track that travelled north to Gersthofen from Oberhausen, lay the scattered, blackened wreckage of the bomber. Among the debris, almost hidden in the grass, she found a leather flying boot. A mist of tears came to her eyes, through which she seemed to see the pilot's face. She carefully laid down the boot and, weeping, walked away.

The young type-setter, Karl-Heinz Meinecke, had been pedalling up the Ulmer Strasse when the sound of the alarm and of the bombers' engines had simultaneously reached him. He had not thought of taking shelter (a reaction which he shared with most of Augsburg), but had stood and watched the aircraft flying low above the town. He had guessed their height to be between 60 and 80 metres, and had known that they were British from the roundels on their sides. There had been the crackle and the banging of the guns – he had seen the tracer-bullets arc across the sky – and then the boom of heavy bombs. One of the bombers, flaming like a meteor, had roared overhead and disappeared behind the buildings at the west end of the street. Karl-Heinz had promptly jumped upon his bicycle and hurried in pursuit. Twenty minutes later, he cycled underneath the railway bridge at Vogelsang and turned right on the road for Schilpsheim. There lay the bomber, on its belly in a meadow. Karl-Heinz set his bicycle against the hedge and cautiously moved closer. There was no sign of fire, but smoke hung in the air. Four men were standing near the nose – standing as though waiting – and a fifth lay at their feet. Karl-Heinz gazed at the great wings of the aircraft, at the engines with their bent propeller blades, the long, deep fuselage, still wreathed in wisps of smoke and torn across the middle like a pulled Christmas cracker. He read the painted letters 'KM A'. Then, near the tail – and this was when the flesh beneath his scalp began to creep – he saw an arm, a charred and blackened arm, pointing straight up at the sky.

Soldiers came, and took the airmen at the nose away. More soldiers, wearing rubber aprons, searched in the fuselage and collected what they found in canvas bags. Karl-Heinz cycled slowly back to Augsburg.

Johann Wagner, having prudently awaited the 'All Clear', came on the scene a little later. From the balcony of the Kriegshaber apartment, he had watched the aircraft make their bombing runs at a height he judged to be below a hundred metres, some two kilometres away, and he had stayed there, watching, shocked but fascinated, with his hands over his ears. He had seen one bomber falling on the skyline, like a ball of flame, and, through the smoke and dust around the factory, had seen a great hole blasted in the wall. Later, when the cacophony of engines, guns and bombs had died away, a man below him in the street had shouted out that one bomber was down at Emersacker and another near to Schilpsheim – that one would be within his cycle-range.

The fallen bomber seemed undamaged from a distance, but when he ventured closer – the guard did not prevent him – he realised that the fuselage was broken. He could see from one end to the other, as though through a telescope, and concluded that whatever or whoever that fuselage had held must have been entirely burned away. The thought that came into the mind of twelve-year-old Johann, on the day which brought his first experience of war, was 'What a tragedy!'

At the plant, the M.A.N. technicians were checking on the damage. This looked pretty bad, as to the fabric of the buildings (and did so later in the recce photographs): the roof of the assembly shed was full of holes, the largest being some eighty feet across, and the upper floor was wrecked; one of the grinding shops was badly knocked about; the other, and two adjacent sheds, were damaged; a shattered bridge would have to be demolished, and not a single window-pane remained intact. But to the plant itself the harm was less than catastrophic: of 2,700 machine-tools, eight were destroyed, sixteen badly damaged and fifty-three had some degree of damage: of 558 cranes, five were destroyed, six badly damaged. One bomb, a 'near miss' on the assembly shed, had smashed through a gate and slid along the main works road without exploding; that made five, of seventeen to hit the factory, which failed to detonate. Four more bombs had hit the textile works just to the east of M.A.N., and caused some casualties there. In all, twelve people had been killed, two of them women, and roughly twice as many injured.

In achieving this, three Lancasters went down, sixteen airmen lost their lives and five would spend the next three years as prisoners of war. These, when added to the toll of JG 2, made Augsburg's cost seem high; not perhaps in terms of lives – that loss, though sore enough for those who were to mourn in Britain and South Africa, in Canada and New Zealand, was small compared with many casualty lists – but seven Lancasters of twelve would never fly or fight again, seven of the tiny force at Harris's disposal. Nor, as cynics on the Squadrons had suspected and as Lord Selborne's experts would be quick to underline, did the assembly-shop of Maschinenfabrik Augsburg-Nürnberg Aktiengesellschaft turn out to be all that much of a bottleneck: five plants in Germany and France, it so transpired, were making Diesel engines as licensed satellites of M.A.N., and the hiatus in production would be eventually assessed by Hitler's specialists as 'slight'. No queues of powerless U-boats would lie immobile in construction-yards at Hamburg, Kiel or Bremen; the deadly war in the Atlantic would not pause. What effects the raid might have would lie elsewhere – in German hearts and minds. For those of Hitler's hierarchy who really thought about the future pattern of the war, and certainly for Augsburgers, it was significant that any Allied bomber – so lightly armed and unprotected – could penetrate so far, and not at night, but in the good light of an April afternoon; for those with eyes to see, the message of the Augsburg raid was written on the wall – that some day soon no corner of the Fatherland would be secure from heavy bombers, night or day.

94

7

The Homeward Highway

The men who flew the bombers on the westward route for home – Nettleton alone of 44, and the two surviving pairs of 97's six – were not considering the future conduct of the war. Their concern was not with strategy, but tactics, and the business of 'flying right'. The tactics, until then, had not been theirs to choose: they had simply flown the way that they were briefed, and done what had been asked of them. It had been, as they would say, 'a rather shaky do'. Now they were concerned in nothing but to nurse their wounded Lancasters along the tracks that led to Lincolnshire, welcoming the night that slowly overtook them, spreading like a blanket from the east. That, and try to keep their minds on track, as well.

Nettleton, well ahead and south of all the rest, had lost faith in his master gyro-compass, and was trying to fly the course that Sands had given him by means of the P4. There were those who wondered later whether all the trouble near Bernay had come about because of a malfunction of that master gyro-compass. It was possible, they thought, that the gyro was put out of true during the time when Nettleton was flying over England ('Very, very bumpy,' Brian Hallows had remarked).

Although the wire cage was meant to prevent the instrument from being knocked about, there was a chance, said some, that the unit could have struck the cage and stuck at such an angle that its readings were misleading from then on.

The readings of the pilot's P4 compass (which lay below the panel on his left) were dictated only by the earth's magnetic field. They were reliable in straight and level flight, provided due account was taken of the influence of metal in the aeroplane itself, and not prone to precession as a gyro-compass was, but the needle wandered madly in any sort of turn, and took a while to settle down again. It was not the easiest of instruments to read at night, nor when you were tired and low on powers of concentration.

Whether for these reasons, or because the air-plot was in error, will never now be known (although B-Baker's crew believed in him, the choice of Sands, who had learned his skills in the skies of Australia, to navigate the leader had caused some mutterings among the Squadron's British-trained observers); the fact was that the aircraft was a long way off its track and ETA. McClure, whose reading of the map had been so useful in the daylight, could now give little help. When at last he saw a coast, the best advice that he could give was that it did not look like France.

* * *

As Penman neared the English coast, he glanced over his shoulder at Y-Yorker's ghostly shape, as he had done many times throughout the homeward flight. For five hundred miles or more since they left Augsburg,

Deverill had kept immaculate formation, judging his position and his distance by the yellow glow that came from U-Uncle's port exhausts. To fly formation in the dark was always difficult, but it was less hard on the leader's right than on his left, because the view was better from the pilot's seat. Why Deverill did not take the starboard station is not possible to say – perhaps he did not like to take the dead man's place – perhaps, because he started on the left, it seemed correct to stay there. Perhaps he never thought of it at all. Now, at any rate, the chore he had imposed on himself was coming to an end. Penman knew that England's coastal defences could not be totally relied on to discriminate between their friends and foes, and that to take evasive action in the dark, in close formation, would not be a sensible idea. He told Deverill to give himself more room, and if necessary, to make his own way back to base.

Either they were unobserved, or identified as friends, for they crossed the coast unchallenged, and began the long descent to Woodhall Spa.

Hallows and Rodley had lost contact after darkness fell, but their airspeeds and their courses were so closely matched that they joined the Woodhall circuit within minutes of each other. Throttled back to hold a thousand feet, with the twinkling line of runway lights to port, Hallows made the downwind checks for landing: '"George" out, super-chargers 'M' gear, air intake 'Cold', brakes off and pressures OK, wheels going down . . .'

The roar of slipstream deepened as the undercarriage doors opened. 'Pitch twenty-eight-fifty,' Hallows ordered, and pushed down with his hand on the wing-flaps lever. 'Flap twenty degrees . . . what the bloody hell!' On his left, the airfield lights had tilted as the Lancaster banked suddenly to port. Instinctively, he knew the reason: when, over the factory, the shell had hit his wing, it must have put the flap on that side out of action, and the starboard flap was giving assymmetric lift. (The flap changed the aerodynamic profile of the wing and lowered the stalling speed; Hallows would normally use a quarter flap for take-off, a third for the approach and all of it for touch-down.) He pulled the lever up and levelled out the wings: this was going to be a landing without flap. He would extend the downwind leg, make a shallow, long approach and, maintaining flying speed, set the wheels down on the runway as close to the threshold as he could.

Rodley, following, made a careful judgment of his distance behind the tiny glow of Hallows's navigation lights. He knew that the Watchtower would not give him landing clearance until the man in front was off the runway, and he did not want to have to go around again (no pilot ever did). He banked on to the crosswind leg, gently losing height and bringing back the speed through 140 to 130 mph. Then, the last swing of the 'spectacles', the last push on the rudders, and the nose came round to line up with the flare-path dead ahead. He pressed the transmit-button. 'Lifebuoy Freddie – funnels, over.'

'F-Freddie, continue your approach. One aircraft ahead, over.'

Rodley lowered more flap and, assisted by his second pilot, made the final checks. 'Wheels down and locked . . .'

'Okay, Rod, lights are green,' confirmed Colquhoun.

'Pitch fully fine . . .'

Colquhoun pulled the levers up against their stops and turned the friction knob. 'Fully fine.'

At the far end of the runway, Hallows's lights moved slowly through a quarter-circle as he steered on to the peri-track, and the voice from the Watchtower came through Rodley's headphones: 'F-Freddie, you're clear to land. Wind zero-six-five, light, over.'

Within half an hour the last two Lancasters were growling overhead, and Penman, in his turn, heard 'Clear to land'. He touched down at ten minutes to midnight, and taxied round the track to his dispersal as Deverill brought Y-Yorker in behind him. He unclipped his face-mask and, opening his window, took a long breath of the cold, sweet air. That always was a time for a pilot to remember, full of sensations and emotions that were hard to analyse. There was the relief of being back, of knowing you had got away with it again. You would soon be eating eggs and bacon, and going to sleep in your own bed. Tomorrow, you would make another entry in your log-book – 'DCO' for 'Duty carried out'. No need yet to think about the next time. Just for now, you were all right. And yet you felt dispirited, a little flat. Perhaps it was a sense of anti-climax. You had been high, and now were low; up there, the mighty aeroplane had soared and banked in answer to your touch: down here, it was a clumsy vehicle, lurching heavily around the corners, while you squeezed brakes and juggled throttles. The sky was limitless; it made all else seem small. You, and the aeroplane, were both somehow diminished.

There were many waiting on the airfield, many, of all ranks – far more than had a duty to be there. Some simply felt the need to see the aircraft land – and the men whom they had thought as good as dead when they took off that afternoon. Some knew it for a moment none who could be there should miss, a moment to remember in the history of the Squadron, of the Station, and part of their experience of war: 'I helped bomb them up', 'I worked on their engines', 'I cooked their breakfast' and 'I saw them land'.

Those who watched and waited heard, with new perception, the quick bark of the Merlins and the squeal of brakes as the bombers were manoeuvred round the field, heard the long roar as the pilots ran the engines down, and the hum of aircrew coaches on the tarmac.

At de-briefing (known then as 'Interrogation', for the word had not yet been debased by connotations of Gestapo cells), senior officers stood by, greeting crews as they came in; smiling WAAFs brought mugs of cocoa and offered packs of cigarettes. The intelligence officers seated them at tables, and asked the usual questions. The aircrews drank the cocoa, smoked the cigarettes, and gave their careful answers, eschewing all heroics, telling of the raid in terms of the essentials – of latitudes and longitudes, of heights and times and speeds.

Penman was surprised to find how kindly people treated him – 'as though they were quite glad to see us' – and Rodley, who had been so determined to return to hearth and home, was struggling to believe he really had. Then, each with his own thoughts and feelings – of satisfaction or elation, of brief unspoken sorrow for the dead, of simple weariness – the crews walked to the messes for their breakfasts, and Woodhall Spa fell silent on that cool, clear April night.

*　　*　　*

In a cottage on the Plaine de St André, Bert Dowty stirred and, waking, could not instantly remember where he was. He turned, felt the warmth of somebody beside him in the bed, and knew: he was far from Waddington. He was, in fact, a non-paying guest of Madame Odette La Sage, who had taken the six men of T-Tommy's crew into her home when, having left the shelter of the woods at dusk, they had knocked upon her door and Birkett had explained their presence in his schoolboy French. Dowty's bed-mate was Saunderson, the wireless operator; Birkett and Dedman shared another double bed; Cobb and Miller had a couch downstairs. Dowty gently prodded Saunderson: 'What time is it, Sandy?' 'No idea. My watch stopped at twelve minutes past five. Go to sleep, Bert, will you? We've got to be away by dawn, before the Krauts come looking.'

In B-Baker, they were very much aware of what the time was – it was time that they were down. At half-an-hour past midnight, with the fuel-tanks nearly dry (and Dorehill's thoughts returning to those pigeons in the back), Nettleton decided with reluctance, for no airman likes admitting he is lost, that the time had come when he must call for help. It was the moment Charlie Churchill had been waiting for – that every wireless operator waited for – the moment when only his skill with the buzzer and the codes could save the aircraft and the crew.

'Wireless Op to Captain – may I use SOS procedure, Sir?'

'Use what you like, just get me a course for home.'

Churchill tapped it out: 'Dit-dit-dit dah-dah-dah dit-dit-dit . . .' The stream of wireless traffic in his head-phones stilled to gentle sibilance. Years afterwards, Churchill was to say that the response was the most beautiful sound that he had ever heard. Gratefully he decoded dots and dashes: 'Aircraft in distress, transmit for bearing on this frequency.' Moments later, he instructed Nettleton: 'Course is zero-seven-five, Sir. They're sending us to Squire's Gate.' Sands was studying the map. 'That's just south of Blackpool, JD. It means we're over the Irish Sea. I'll work out an ETA.'

B-Baker touched down on the diversion airfield a minute before one o'clock in the morning of 18th April, after ten hours in the air. Carrying their gear, Nettleton and his crew came stiffly down the ladder from the fuselage and, standing close together by the towering starboard fin, waited in the darkness as the hooded headlights of a pick-up truck drew near.

In the tower at Waddington, the Watch Office shift had changed. The RT Operator who relieved Pip Beck had heard no call for 'Jetty' from any 'Maypole' aircraft, and she knew now that there would be no call. The fire-truck crew stood down, the lights went out in hangars, offices and locker-rooms, in the armoury and transport sheds, the kitchens and the sick-bay. The long day's wait had ended. The Augsburg raid was over . . .

8

'No Life was Lost in Vain'

On Saturday, 18th April, Royal Air Force Waddington was exceptionally quiet – almost as quiet as it had been before the bombers came, when sheep had grazed the soft, green fields where now the runways lay. One cause of this was simply lack of aeroplanes (of thirteen on establishment, only three were airworthy); another was the sense of shock that hit the men and women of the Station when they came on duty and learned of what had happened to the Squadron's crews. Pip Beck, walking briskly from her quarters to the tower, remarked the silence and, in the Watch Office, found everyone subdued. Then she was told the dreadful news. She was not a hypersensitve girl, and she knew that death was a concomitant of war, but her young heart ached to think of the familiar names on the Battle Order that would not be there again, and of the voices of the pilots that she would hear no more. And, because she was a woman, she thought of all the mothers, sisters, wives and sweethearts whose lives would suffer such a cruel change.

Meanwhile, the Commanding Officer, Group Captain Purdon-Lewis, was writing at his desk in SHQ; at Woodhall Spa, Wing Commander Collier was similarly occupied. The task each officer had set himself was one that did not fall to many men: it was to recommend the King's award of the Victoria Cross. 'The officer,' Purdon-Lewis wrote of Nettleton, 'showed in this action the finest qualities of skilled airmanship, leadership, courage and determination.' Collier wrote 'By extreme devotion to duty, Squadron Leader Sherwood ensured the success of the operation . . . and continued his daring leadership to the end. His conspicuous bravery . . . crowned a long and distinguished career in the service of his country.'

The recommendations were despatched to Grantham for endorsement. There, Group Captain Haines, acting for AOC 5 Group, wrote 'Recommended' under each report, and added to Sherwood's, 'This gallant leadership deserves the highest recognition. His example will always be remembered in this Group and in the Royal Air Force.' At High Wycombe, later that same day, the C-in-C found room to write, 'Strongly recommended, AT Harris, AM' along the bottom of each form, and passed them on to London, where some deity, dwelling on the high slopes of the Air Ministry Olympus, glanced at Sherwood's document and added this condition, in a cooly pencilled scrawl: 'To be recd for DSO if later found to be alive.'

Immediate awards were also sought for others who returned. There would be a DSO for Penman ('He showed great skill in the handling of his section and the greatest determination in attacking the target from a very low level, in spite of intense and accurate anti-aircraft fire'), and DFCs for Hallows ('His leader was shot down in flames . . . he then took over command of the remainder of the section . . . Throughout the whole operation, he showed the greatest possible determination and pluck'); for Deverill ('His aircraft was hit in numerous places causing a fire . . . which burned a large portion of the fuselage'), and for Rodley ('One aircraft failing, he was called on to take part . . .); further DFCs were recommended for the second pilots Dorehill ('He exhibited the greatest calmness and indifference to danger') and Hooey ('He greatly assisted the leader to find and bomb the target by accurate map-reading'), and for the observers Sands ('In spite of attacks and constant evasive action, his navigation was such that the target . . . was reached within a few minutes of the estimated time of arrival'), McClure ('. . . he brought the aircraft in on a dead accurate approach') and Ifould ('By accurate bombing-aiming under intense fire he scored direct hits on the main works').

DFMs were recommended for ten of the NCOs: of Nettleton's crew, Churchill ('He rendered valuable aid in assisting . . . to bring his aircraft safely home'), Huntley ('By accurate fire he discouraged any enemy aircraft from frontal attack on the formation . . .'), Mutter ('He carried out a running commentary of the whole action for the information of the pilot . . . whilst firing his guns in the most determined and calm manner') and Harrison ('He returned the fire until his guns went out of action'), Overton of Penman's crew, Ratcliffe of Rodley's, Louch and Goacher of Hallows's, and of Deverill's crew Irons and Mackay (they 'dealt with the situation with great calmness and resource . . . putting out the fire after it had gained a considerable hold').

Some weeks later, when it was known that they were prisoners-of-war, recommendations would follow for the survivors of A-Apple's crew: the DFC for Garwell ('He exhibited valour, determination, and skill of the highest order'), DFMs for Watson and Dando, and for Kirke ('He has always shown the same courage and indifference to danger') a bar to his DFM.

Sixteen men of 97 Squadron, officers and NCOs, who had been to Augsburg and returned, were not recommended for awards. They would not have worried about that: they knew that 'gongs' were limited, even for such trips as theirs, and would have figured that you either had to be a pilot or do something pretty special to get your name and number on the list. It would be enough for them that they would wake up in their beds at Woodhall Spa tomorrow, and that in their log-books would be written: '17th April 1942 – Augsburg – DCO.'

In the context of awards, 'immediate' was not a literal description: Nettleton and his men would not be marched before the King on Monday morning. The term distinguished their awards, which marked one outstanding feat of arms, from the 'non-immediate' sort bestowed on the survivors of a series of more routine operations and described sometimes by their recipients as 'arriving with the rations'. The Augsburg decorations would not be announced, in fact, until the press reception on 27th April. At that time, the ribbons would be worn but the actual hardware – the crosses and the medals – would not be pinned on chests by George VI until the following September.

The story of the raid itself was issued, by Air Ministry communiqué, on Saturday 18th April – in good time for the Sunday nationals to make it headline news. 'WAR'S MOST DARING RAID', proclaimed The People, and continued: 'As details of the Lancaster are still secret, it is impossible to estimate the load of bombs taken to Augsburg. In any case, such a long flight, in which speed was essential, would make it impossible for the bombers to carry anything near their maximum load . . . The target is of such vital importance in the Battle of the Atlantic that even a reasonable prospect of success amply justified the certainty of heavy casualties being incurred . . .'

On that same Saturday, another daylight mission had been flown, on the far side of the world. Taking off from aircraft carriers, and led by Colonel Jimmy Doolittle, a force of USAAF B25s had given Tokyo its baptism of fire. The Sunday Pictorial proclaimed the 'Greatest week of bombing in the history of war' beneath the banner headlines 'AMAZING DAY RAID BY THE RAF', and commented '. . .assuming that the bombers got squarely on the proper target – and they could hardly miss – the loss of seven aircraft was well worthwhile . . .' (The fortitude with which some sections of the Press accepted casualties did not go unremarked by fighting men.)

'AUGSBURG SUCCESS', The Sunday Observer announced, 'OUR NEW BOMBERS USED – DIESEL WORKS DAMAGED', and added soberly: 'It must be remembered, however, that in so rapid an attack, although it is possible for the crews to see their bombs burst, they have little chance of making more than a tentative estimate of the damage caused . . .'

The damage to the bombers was also being assessed: Nettleton's B-Baker could not be ferried back from Lancashire until those strange grooves in the wings had been examined, and all four Lancasters at Woodhall Spa had either flak holes or hydraulic punctures – and some had both – to be repaired. As for the aircrew, they were confined to duties on the ground until the time should come when they were called to meet the press.

In fulfilment of its function, and in the interests of morale, it was the practice of the Information Ministry to let the people hear, from time to time, the story of an exploit as related by its hero or, perhaps, its heroine, in strict anonymity over the radio. Such broadcasts were of short duration – five minutes at the most – and tended (understandably, in the stringent circumstances of the early nineteen-forties) to exemplify a stiffish upper lip. As individual impressions of the action they comprised, if not the whole truth of the matter, probably the truth and nothing but. John Nettleton made such a broadcast to the nation, following the news on Sunday evening.

As always, he spoke quietly and carefully, in that clipped, English style which would have served as a model for any actor playing an Air Force squadron leader. 'I wish you could see these huge aircraft of ours,' he said. 'There were people in England who did see us flying low overhead on Friday afternoon on our way to Augsburg. We Lancaster crews believe that in the Lancaster we have got the answer for heavy bombing, just as the Stirling, Halifax and Wellington crews believe in their own aircraft. We have tremendous confidence in everything about the Lancaster, and in the workers who are turning them out in such numbers.

'We did the job. I don't feel myself in any doubt about that. But we suffered serious losses in doing it. I was leading the formation which was unlucky enough to run into a large number of German fighters as we were crossing France. Our other formation got through to the target without being attacked at all, but four of my Squadron were shot down one after the other. There isn't very much to be said about that. The best thing is to think about the merchant seamen who won't now be torpedoed, because we have bombed those sheds where the submarine engines are built. My gunners didn't let the enemy get off scot-free, but the most important thing in evading the fighters was to fly as low as you possibly could. I flew no higher than twenty-five feet, following the contours of the ground. You can imagine what it must have been like: thirty tons or so of aircraft, its four engines roaring, driving along at several miles a minute. Horses and cattle in the field scattered in front of us. We saw two German officers out riding; the horses bolted and were still out of control when we last saw them. But the big moment for me was when we came over a hilltop in Germany and saw the roofs and chimneys of Augsburg in front of us, then the buildings of the Diesel engine works, then the big T-shaped shed of the submarine engine building plant.

'There it was. I am confident that our heavy bombs went into it. The remaining Lancaster of my formation was set on fire by the flak as we were running up, but that did not prevent him from dropping his bombs as carefully and accurately as if he had not been ablaze. And this applies to the two aircraft of the other formation which were lost over the target, though all the eight aircraft which reached Augsburg found the works and bombed them, none from higher than three hundred feet. Both captains and their crews whose aircraft were blazing, and who none the less carried on and bombed, did something that everyone can be proud of.

'I think the main thing in all our minds both before and now, after the operation, is that the war cannot be finished without attacking the enemy. We know there are bound to be losses in such attacks, but today we have the right aircraft. We know that we are only sent to attack the most worthwhile targets. We believe that the way to win the war is to have our own Spring offensive before Hitler has his, and in places not of his choice but of ours.'

Given the choice, Bert Dowty would not have spent that Sunday night in Normandy. He would have rather been at home, or Waddington, or anywhere in England. If he had to be in France, he would rather not be stumbling through a forest in the dark. Madame La Sage was clearly getting on in years (it turned out she was all of twenty-three to his nineteen) and she had a husband, even older, who was a distant prisoner-of-war. Nevertheless, it had occurred to him that to stay beneath her roof might not be too terrible an exile. True, she had been warned by neighbours that the presence of her guests, if discovered, would bring harsh reprisals, but she would have sheltered them again the second night – having opened all the windows to remove the trace of Saunderson's tobacco – had they not decided to move on, as much for her sake as their own. All night they had travelled through the woodland west of Conche, lain low during daylight and emerged on Sunday evening near the hamlet La Gueroulde. The faintest glimmer from a doorway had led them to another cottage, 'Le Pilier Vert', the home of Madame Giroux. They had been given bread and soup and coffee; Madame had killed, plucked and drawn a chicken, boiled it while they rested, and wrapped it up in paper and a checkered kerchief to sustain them on their way.

Then, it had been the woods again, with Dowty carrying the precious fowl, moving slowly west toward the railway line that ran south from Alencon. While

Nettleton was speaking on the radio at home, Dowty's face was being scratched by twigs and branches for the thousandth time. 'Press on, Bert,' Birkett had whispered, 'We've done twelve miles so far – only another two hundred and sixty to Bordeaux.' At that moment, Dowty's choice, had he been free of all the bonds that held a crew together, would have been to let them go, sit down, and eat that chicken.

They did not know that earlier that day, a few miles to the north, their captain, alone, his mind still more on Beckett's fate than on his own, had been arrested. Crum was now a prisoner-of-war.

Meanwhile, the daily papers picked up where the Sunday press left off. The Daily Mail ('LANCASTERS HEDGE-HOP ACROSS EUROPE') commented: 'The continued demands of Von Runstedt and the other Nazi defence chiefs for air power to meet the RAF's challenge are causing powerful German air forces to be withheld from other theatres. Russia's recent marked successes in the air against the Germans on the Eastern front are in no small way due to the British pressure from the West. And the great German forces based on the Mediterranean for a spring putsch towards the Suez Canal are still held immobile . . .' From another page the face of Sherwood ('Missing in Raid on Augsburg') gazed out with narrowed eyes. The Daily Express selected Sandford for its 'Missing' photograph, and the story of Nelson, his adopted dog – 'waiting for the sound of a familiar step and the voice that would send him bounding with delight. His vigil was in vain.' (Thirteen months later, this example of the reporter's art would find an echo, albeit with the fates of the participants inverted, in the tale of Wing Commander

Guy Gibson's 'Nigger', run over and killed outside the gates of Scampton while his master led 617 Squadron on the dam-busting raid.)

The Daily Sketch, beneath the heading 'Augsburg Raiders As a German Saw Them', featured a 'composite picture' of eight heavy bombers flying in pairs above Lake Constance. (That Stirlings were depicted was attributed by some to the well-known unreliability of the average eye-witness, but as photographs of the Lancaster had yet to be officially released it seems likely that the Sketch had merely exercised a little journalistic licence.)

'A senseless propaganda exercise', was how the German Information Ministry described the raid. 'The damage done in this attack to our war economy, causing an interruption of production in one factory for a few days, was paid for with the loss altogether of eight new four-engined aeroplanes and fifty personnel . . .' (That the claim exceeded fact by only one, both as to aircraft and to men, was pretty mild by Dr Goebbels's standards. The 'fifty personnel' could not be more than guesswork for, after all, an unknown number of T-Tommy's crew were still at large. The extra bomber claimed could be attributed to the tendency – by no means confined to the German High Comand – to exaggerate success, or to the fact, just possibly, that someone watching Waddington had reported 'No returns'.)

For his part, Mr Churchill took a brighter view of the attack than Dr Goebbels had, and imparted this immediately to the Bomber C-in-C. 'We must plainly regard the attack of the Lancasters,' he signalled, 'on the U-boat factory at Augsburg as an outstanding achievement of the RAF. Undeterred by heavy losses at the outset, the bombers pierced in broad daylight into the heart of Germany, and struck a vital point with deadly precision. Pray convey the thanks of His Majesty's Government to the officers and men who accomplished this memorable feat of arms in which no life was lost in vain.'

The Chief of Air Staff signalled: 'I would like 44 and 97 Squadrons to know the great importance I attach to their gallant and successful attack on the Diesel engine factory at Augsburg. Please give them my warmest congratulations and thanks.'

Relaying these messages to Waddington and Woodhall, Air Marshal Harris added his own sentiments, and did not attempt to hide his pleasure and his pride: 'The resounding blow which has been struck at the enemy's submarine and tank building programme will echo round the world. The full effects on his submarine campaign cannot be immediately apparent, but nevertheless they will be enormous. The gallant adventure penetrating deep into the heart of Germany in daylight and pressed with outstanding determination in the face of bitter and foreseen opposition takes its place amongst the most courageous operations of the war. It is, moreover, yet another fine example of effective co-operation with the other Services by striking at the very sources of enemy effort. The officers and men who took part, those who returned and those who fell, have indeed deserved well of their country.'

The last word lay with Admiral Sir Dudley Pound, the Chief of Naval Staff, who waited for some days before he made this signal to the Bomber Chief: 'I have now seen the photographs and assessment. I am sure this attack will have greatly helped in achieving our objective. I much deplore the comparatively heavy casualties but I feel sure their loss was not in vain.'

In Augsburg itself, reaction varied. While the local Nazi party leaders bent their energies to arranging a public memorial service for the dead in the Elias Holl Platz, the raid was endlessly debated at the factory, both by the workers and the gunners who had so steadfastly defended them. Lukas Kiermeyr, who had attended to the injured in the sheds and seen them on their way to hospital, made his own position clear about the bomber crews. 'They were courageous, yet correct,' he said. 'They could have fired on the people in the streets, but they did not. I would have tended them, those who came down, according to the Geneva Convention. The question of friend or foe does not arise, when a man is wounded.'

The circle in which Karl-Heinz Meinecke moved had quickly seen the implications: 'If they are able to arrive so easily, in broad daylight, it looks bad for us.' At the glider school, there was some open admiration of the venture: 'A real dare-devil piece of flying, all right, if not particularly successful'. There was general surprise that the raid had developed from the south – 'the wrong direction' – and one firm body of opinion was that the bombers must have taken off from Switzerland: 'How else could they have flown so far unhindered?' Johann Wagner, on the other hand, had found no-one with whom to share his great experience, no school-friend or acquaintance who had seen, or even heard, the British bombers.

At 5.30 am on Monday 20th April, before the paper boys began their rounds in England, the men of

T-Tommy's crew were enjoying the luxury of walking in the open. They had meant to lie up in the woods again as soon as it grew light, but their progress on the roads was so comparatively easy that they kept going – just too long. A solitary woman cycled by, and gave a long, suspicious stare. They hurried back into the trees and went to ground. At ten o'clock, the sound of breaking twigs woke Dowty from his doze. He had no need to wake the others; the shrill blast of a whistle saw to that. They were surrounded by police. The officer – the 'Chef' – looked them over carefully, set two gendarmes on guard, and went away.

'That's buggered it,' said Saunderson.

'They'll hand us over to the Krauts.'

'Any of that chicken left, Bert?'

'You had the last of it.'

'Okay, it'll have to be the flying ration chocolate . . .'

The officer came briskly through the trees. 'It appears,' he said, 'that you are not the bandit gang of which we had report. You are free to go.' They rose, scarcely believing their luck. Nodding to his men, the officer turned away, then paused and spoke over his shoulder. 'I recommend the next forest – three kilometres in that direction. Go! Quickly!'

John Nettleton, on leave in London five weeks later (and by then CO of 44 Squadron), moved as quickly as T-Tommy's crew in the Collines de Perche. He was introduced to Betty Havelock of the WAAF Directorate at a cocktail party on 25th May and, when the party ended, she allowed him to escort her to her quarters. The evening was exceptionally warm, and she suggested that he might remove his greatcoat.

'I'd rather not,' he said. 'People recognise the VC ribbon, and ask for one's autograph.'

Within four days, he had proposed (in 'The 400' Club) and been accepted, had taken her to Waddington and introduced her to the Squadron. In the Sergeants' Mess, the senior Warrant Officer imparted his decision after a glass or two of alcohol and due deliberation. 'It's all right, Sir,' he told Nettleton, 'you can marry her.'

9

And Then the Whirlwind

Why the Lancasters came on the target 'in broad daylight' remains a mystery. Ops Order No 143 had stated that 'by making the attack at dusk the return journey can be made under cover of darkness', and again '"Zero hour" (the time for coast crossing) will be calculated on the day of the operation in the light of the meteorological forecast in order to allow the force to attack their target during the last 15 minutes of daylight.'

But navigators did not think of evening visibility in terms of 'daylight', 'dusk' or 'darkness'. They recognised instead three sorts of twilight – 'civil', 'nautical' and 'astronomical'. In the first of these, the horizon can be clearly seen although the sun is six degrees below it, and you can work without the use of artificial light. In nautical twilight, when the sun has sunk another six degrees, the horizon is no longer visible and you do need artificial light. Astronomical twilight begins when the sun is eighteen degrees below the horizon: the sky will then be dark enough for you to see the stars. As the sun takes four minutes to move through one degree, twilight of one sort or another lasts for forty-eight minutes.

The Ops Order's reference to 'dusk' seemed to indicate some time within the civil twilight limits – although that could have varied, depending on the local covering of cloud, by half an hour or more. Given a clear sky, however, (and the forecast promised that), and knowing the moment when the sun was down by six degrees, it was not too hard a calculation to subtract the journey time from that to find the hour at which the bombers should set course.

But then account had to be taken of the difference in longitude – 11 degrees from west to east – which meant that twilight, of whatever sort, would fall on Augsburg almost three-quarters of an hour before it fell on Lincoln, and also of the fact that clocks in Britain were all set on Double Summer Time, to gain two hours of daylight in the evenings of which the early-rising Germans had no need.

In later years, such calculations would be taken in a navigator's stride, but at that time the art, if not in its infancy, was at best in early childhood. If there were errors in the timing of the raid which added to the problems of the pilots flying home, at least they did not add to loss of life.

Many lives were lost, however, and the strength of the attack was seriously reduced, by the inability of the air gunners to fight off JG 2, and this was largely due to the weakness of their weapons. Not only was the Browning's range inadequate for combat with the German fighters, but its performance was, by any standards, poor. Only one Lancaster returned to England with its main defensive armament – the rear and upper turrets – in an operational condition, and several guns had stoppages the gunners could not clear from the first time that the triggers were depressed.

The C-in-C, writing as Marshal of the RAF Sir Arthur Harris some years after the war, was savagely to criticise the 'irresponsible and very often operationally ignorant officials in places like the Ministry of Aircraft Production' who, he believed, frustrated for years his efforts to obtain .5 inch guns for one turret at least in every bomber – a gun with twice the range and weight of fire of .303. Only by acting on his own initiative and unofficially (not, perhaps, a wholly unexampled action in the C-in-C's career), did he eventually procure – from a private family concern of engineers – the turret he was seeking.

In their next 'Analysis of Operations', submitted by routine to Bomber Command HQ, 5 Group's Air Staff tersely gave the facts and figures, as they knew them, of the operation known as 'Margin': 'Successful and Returned – 5 (41.7%), Missing Before Bombing – 4 (33.3%), Missing After Bombing – 3 (25%).' Concerning the diversionary attack, the report exposed, without comment, the discrepancy in timing between the plan made at High Wycombe and the deed: 'These aircraft . . .(the 2 Group Bostons) . . .being above the target approximately 30 minutes before the Lancasters crossed the coast.' (Order No 143 had read 'Z minus 10'). The German fighters were described as 'About 30 Me 109s and FW 190s', which was in accord with Nettleton's report, but not with the Luftwaffe records. These showed that JG 2 did not begin to re-equip with Focke-Wulfe 190s until a month after the raid. Inexperienced as B-Baker's gunners were, and unused to seeing German fighters as were all the crew by light of day, it was remarkable that they should take the long, sleek, in-line engine of the Messerschmitt for the

119

FW 190's radial, with its distinctive, rounded cowling. But, as every man who flew in combat would acknowledge, mistakes in recognition were the norm, not the exception. Furthermore, Crum's gunners had thought they saw two FW 190s fly by while they were trying to burn T-Tommy near Bernay, so there may have been a few of them around.

The 5 Group Analysis concluded that, although the fighter interception near Bernay was probably a chance encounter, the Lancasters needed to be armed with bigger guns if they were going to operate by day; that thirty-minute delay fuses on the bombs would 'allow aircraft to break formation over the target and attack independently from different directions' (this, it was suggested, would confuse the ground defences and prevent them from concentrating on one line of approach); and, lastly, that the bomber crews, before a daylight operation, should practise their evasive tactics with friendly fighter aircraft.

The OR people at High Wycombe, compiling the 'Bomber Command Report on Operations' on 5th May, dealt more fully, and more harshly, with the diversionary efforts of 17th April than the 5 Group staff had done. 'Since the Lancasters', they wrote, under the heading Subsidiary Operations as Diversions, 'were intercepted and severely handled by enemy fighters it appears that the main purpose of these raids was not achieved . . .' continuing, 'Although much enemy fighter activity occurred throughout the day there were comparatively few engagements and losses were slight on both sides. Thus the enemy was maintained in a constant state of alert without being exhausted . . .the diversion front, extending from Calais to Cherbourg, embraced the route taken by the Lancasters. If it was hoped that the enemy reporting system would be thus saturated this hope was not realised and it appears probable that far from drawing off the enemy fighter strength the subsidiary operations brought about the reinforcement of the Le Havre area.'

It was to be a different story when the bombers went to Augsburg nearly two years later. By then, equipment had accumulated and technique had developed on a massive scale, and it was a massive force that carried out the raid. Almost six hundred aircraft were to set out on the evening of 25th February 1944, of which a hundred odd were Pathfinders to find and light the target, the rest being Main Force heavies with two thousand tons of HE and incendiary bombs. They would be assisted by devices, quite unknown in 1942, such as H2S, to give a rudimentary television picture of the ground below; such as Monica and Boozer, to warn the pilot of a night fighter's approach; such as Mandrel, which would interfere with early warning radar; and such as Airborne Cigar and Tinsel, to jam the fighters' radio control. While they were on their way, twenty-four Mosquitoes would be striking other targets – Mannheim, Aachen, Schweinfurt and Saarbrucken – and hitting fighter airfields in the Netherlands and Belgium. As an additional diversion, more than a hundred fledgling bomber crews would be laying sea-mines off the coast at St. Nazaire and in the waters north of Kiel. That the attack should be delivered in the dark, despite its strength, would show how well the lesson had been learned – since April 1942 no heavy bomber of the RAF was to fly so far in daylight, nor would thereafter, not until the Luftwaffe, to all intents and purposes, had been denied the sky. The heavy bombers' aiming point was not to be the factory, but in the centre of the town, for times and strategies had changed. Knock down the workers' houses, smash their roads, gas mains and power supply, destroy their transport and their sewerage systems, terrorise their families – why bother with their works? And anyway, with that enormous tonnage going down from 20,000 feet, many bombs would hit the factory fortuitously – many more than 44 and 97 aimed at such a cost.

Augsburg was to suffer dreadful hurt. That would be the price to pay for total war. 'They sowed the wind,' the C-in-C had said, 'Now they will reap the whirlwind.' It did not matter that such seeds as the merchant, Jakob Fugger, and his family had sown back in the 16th century were never meant for evil, but for good – they were the seeds of a benevolent society, and of a great estate, a peaceful haven for the poor in their old age, the oldest social housing project in the world. But that could not be spared in total war, no more than Hermann Goering's bombers spared the treasures of the cities they attacked. So the Fuggerei, and many another piece of history, would be destroyed. Years later, Lukas Kiermeyr would say: 'After the first raid, we asked ourselves, "Will it get worse?" It got worse, all right.' Karl Dömling's view would be: 'M.A.N. was a war objective – that raid was legitimate. The later raid was different.' And Johann Wagner: 'We just had to live through it, if we could.'

Not that the force of 1944 would have an easy ride. The backroom boys in Germany would find a way to counter all the new advances in their turn. They would give the fighters 'Flensburg', to home on Monica and

122

Boozer, and 'Naxos', to do the same with H2S. They would develop 'Wuerzburg' – a precision radar – to direct the searchlights and the flak, and give the fighters upward-firing cannon – 'Schraege Musik' – to exploit the blind spot in the heavy bomber gunners' field of vision. And the Luftwaffe would counteract the jamming of their radio by sending 109s and Focke-Wulfes – day fighter aircraft – to use the searchlights' guidance high above the target in seeking out their prey. Such a fighter was a 'Wilde Sau': the 'Zahme Sau', or tame boar, was an orthodox night fighter, sent to prowl, in mass, among the bomber stream.

Almost a hundred of the mighty bomber force, for one reason or another, would not drop their bombs on Augsburg, and twenty-one would not return. Nevertheless, the operation, which was directed in two phases, one on either side of midnight, would be regarded as a tactical success. Great fires would burn, from which the smoke was to ascend 12,000 feet, while vast explosions shook the night, and the glow of flames would still be seen two hundred miles away, from bombers flying home. Amid that holocaust, specific damage to the engine factory was not to merit mention in the Ops Analysis.

By the time of this attack, T-Tommy's crew had been prisoners for nearly twenty months. Cobb and Miller had been captured near to Châteauroux; Dedman, Birkett, Saunderson and Dowty had been arrested barely a hundred miles short of their haven while travelling with their guide and mentor, Francis Gagnard of Alençon, on the train from Limoges to Bordeaux. Always the forager, Bert Dowty had acquired two kilograms of butter on the way. He had lost that, with his freedom. The evaders had been returned to Evreux airfield under guard, had dutifully given name, rank and number to their interrogator, and been transported, via Paris, to a fortress prison in the Alpes Maritimes.

Gagnard himself, grieving at the loss of his RAF flock, had continued with his own plan of action – to join the Free French Air Force in North Africa. This, despite a spell of imprisonment in Spain, he had achieved (and pursued successfully enough to earn the Croix de Guerre and Medaille Militaire).

Early in September 1942, the six men of T-Tommy's crew had joined a mass escape of fifty-eight POWs, over half of whom had stayed at large despite all efforts by the Garde Mobile to hunt them down, and eventually reached England via the escape route known as 'The Pat O'Leary Line'. T-Tommy's men, less fortunate, had been recaptured after one precarious night of freedom in the mountains, and removed to stricter custody in Italy. Birkett had been transferred to a special camp for South Africans and Rhodesians (Birkett having foresworn his nationality and adopted Dedman's for the purpose). Then, when the Allies threatened Italy, Saunderson and Dowty had been moved to Germany and, on 25th February 1944, were inmates of Stalag 11a, some thirty miles to the west of Magdeburg. There, Dowty's lucky star, sometimes a fickle light, had shone on him again: he had been befriended by a Belgian who, with other French-speakers, worked in the Stalag Post Office outside the main compound and enjoyed a better life-style and cuisine than British prisoners. These extra rations, Bert Dowty would be making his covert way to share (leaving Saunderson his share of skilly), as was his practice every evening after roll-call, when the bombers flew to Augsburg once again.

David Penman (who had taken off for Augsburg as a carefree Flight Lieutenant and returned to bear the burdens of an Acting Squadron Leader) took the opportunity, while grounded to await the press reception, to call on Sherwood's wife – to tell her what had happened at the factory and to offer such condolences as he could put in words. But Mrs Sherwood had no need of these, for she was sure her husband had survived. In due course, when it was known that she was right, the scrawled condition of the Kingsway potentate applied – Sherwood's DSO was promulgated. For her part, Mrs Sherwood was content; better John Sherwood DSO for a husband than John Sherwood VC dead.

Except for one or two – perhaps the VC and the CGM – honours and awards were not particularly coveted nor held in special, high regard by the majority of airmen; nor, in the last analysis, at the midnight of man's day in the millenia of history, would any medal matter very much. But they had their significance, some meaning in society, as an overt recognition by the State of services which went beyond the simple call of duty. They could be a source of pride to friends and relatives, and might bring the recipient an afterglow to warm his later life.

There were those who said that Mycock should have had a high award, and that only the VC would meet the case – indeed there was no other decoration for the dead. Mycock's conduct over Augsburg appeared to go officially unmarked, but he would be remembered as a very valiant airman by everyone who knew about the raid.

Others of the dead were 'Mentioned in Dispatches',

their names recorded in the London Gazette and next-of-kin informed. Arthur Cox's father, for example, received a letter from Brian Hallows (himself a Squadron Leader now, like David Penman, and acting for the OC 97 Squadron) on 5th January 1943. 'The King', wrote Hallows, 'has been graciously pleased to give orders for the name of your son to be published as Mentioned in Dispatches by the Air Officer Commanding-in-Chief. You will receive the Certificate in due course. This award was made for the gallant part your son took in the attack on Augsburg last year.'

Arthur's mother, some months later, received a letter-card from Germany: 'Dear Mrs Cox. There is little I can tell you of the actual flight to Augsburg owing to my present position. Your son was killed when we crashed and is buried near Augsburg in Bavaria, which is very beautiful country in Southern Germany. I do not remember much about the crash myself but the rest of my crew must have been killed instantly. Yours sincerely, J.S. Sherwood, S/L.'

The card had been written in Stalag Luft 3. It was dated 17th April 1943, the Augsburg anniversary.

Five years later, Mr Cox was informed, by an Air Ministry letter, that the remains of sixteen airmen had been recovered from their graves in the environs of Augsburg and reinterred in the British Military Cemetery at Bad Tolz, south of Munich. The body of his son, one of seven which could be identified, now lay in Grave 4, Row G, Plot 6. 'I do sincerely hope', ran the letter, 'the knowledge that your son's last resting place, with those of his comrades surrounding it, will always be reverently tended, may be of some slight comfort to you.'

The letter was not dissimilar to the one Mr Cox had

126

received a few years earlier, about his younger son. In June 1944, John too had died in battle, while serving with the Gordon Highlanders in France.

The 97 Squadron pilots who returned to Woodhall Spa flew many further operations, and all survived the war (Penman, indeed, and Rodley continued flying for many years, as did Dorehill of 44), but their Lancasters did not. Penman's U-Uncle, Hallows's B-Baker and Rodley's F-Freddie, in the hands of other pilots, were lost within the following few months; even Deverill's Y-Yorker, though actually taken out of combat and put out to grass at Wigsley HCU, was seen to break up in the air while flying over Hertfordshire in 1943. But while Nettleton's B-Baker flew on throughout the war – indeed, until consignment to the scrap-yard came in 1947 – he himself, did not. Soon after Augsburg, he received the acting rank of Wing Commander, along with the command of 44. With the help of a benevolent WAAF Directorate and her own persuasive powers, Betty Havelock contrived a posting to the RCAF night fighter airfield at Coleby Grange, just three miles down the Sleaford Road from Waddington. When his aircrews were on 'stand-down' Nettleton would visit, sometimes to discuss tactics with the Canadian Commanders of the three Beaufighter Squadrons, always to lunch with Betty. His flying was more restricted now, as was that of all the bomber squadron COs, and he had to pick the missions he would fly on. Being the man he was, he picked the tough ones: no 'Gardening', no short range trips, for Nettleton.

'When they give you the VC,' he confided to Betty, 'it's like giving a dog a bad name in reverse. You have to go on all the stinkers, or people would say you were resting on your laurels. The trouble is you never know what's coming up until Group send the order through. It's like doing your first op all over again.'

The part of the job that distressed him most – so Betty discovered – was the all-too-frequent need to be the bearer, by letter or in person, of the worst news in the world: the news that a husband or a son would not be coming home.

To illustrate the sort of commander that he set himself to be, a single incident will serve. One night, in between the briefing and the time for take-off, a pilot decided that he did not want to fly. Many a commander would have simply called for the reserve. Nettleton, however, climbed into the cabin and took the Lancaster and the defaulter's crew to Germany himself. (That unhappy man, who had a history of abortive sorties, was subsequently court-martialled for 'lack of moral fibre').

John Nettleton and Betty Havelock were married in Lincoln on 17th July 1942, at the Church of St Mary Magdalen, conveniently close – for the reception – to the best-appointed hostelry in Lincoln. The RAF padre from Waddington assisted the Vicar in the conduct of the service.

At the end of his tour, Nettleton took the shortest possible 'rest' at a Heavy Conversion Unit and hurried to rejoin the Squadron – now based at Dunholme Lodge, some five miles north of Lincoln.

On 12th July 1943, Turin was the target – the first in a brief concentration on Italian cities by the bombers, intended to combine with the Allied armies' assault from the south in encouraging an early surrender from Rome. The mission was not thought to be particularly hazardous. A long ride but, as operations went, 'a piece

128

of cake', and to see the Alps by moonlight was a marvellous experience. The route was planned to take the bombers out over the Bay of Biscay and across the south of France, avoiding all the best-defended areas.

Nettleton, originally, had not been on the battle order. indeed, he had arranged to lunch next day at Coleby Grange. It happened that he was having trouble with his ears – serious enough for the specialist, within the past few days, to say that he must give up flying for a while. This advice he begged should not be pressed until his second tour of operations was complete. It may be he determined then to fly as often as he could before the doctors insisted on his grounding. He took off for Turin with a typical Wing Commander's crew: ad hoc, made up of section leaders and 'spare bods'.

The customary pre-lunch drinks at Coleby Grange on 13th July seemed to Betty Nettleton to go on far too long. She phoned through to Dunholme Lodge: Wing Commander Nettleton was 'not available'. The Canadians rallied round: 'Probably landed away, short on gas . . .', 'Could be down in the drink – they'll pick him up OK . . .' Then she was called to the telephone: John's Station Commander was on his way to see her. She knew well enough what task Group Captain Leonard Slee had set himself.

Opinion on the Squadron was that their Commander, on the homeward route, had somehow strayed above the guns of Brest (in the early hours of 13th July, a Lancaster with three engines on fire had been reported going into the sea). His was the only aircraft lost of fourteen sent that night from Dunholme Lodge.

In February 1944, that same month in which the Harris whirlwind swept through Augsburg, John's son was born to Betty Nettleton.

*   *   *

Two years after he had led the Messerschmitts of Jagdgeschwader 2 against Nettleton's Lancasters, Walter Oesau – now commanding JG1 – got into a scrap with some USAAF P38s ('Lightnings' to the RAF). By then, his tally of aircraft destroyed was a hundred and twenty-five. On the 11th May 1944, high above the place where H-Howe's ashes lay, Oberst Oesau, Knight's Cross with oak leaves and swords, German fighter pilot, fought his last fight.

For Dowty and Saunderson, the struggle continued. At Stalag 11a they had fallen out with the authorities, who required them to carry out labouring tasks. This, they declined to do. The fact that they had the Geneva Convention on their side did not cut much ice. Handcuffed together, with a score of like-minded prisoners, they were packed off to a camp in Poland, where the conditions set new standards in austerity. Their eventual escape and homeward march, in April 1945, deserve a story to themselves.

10
The only way . . .

There is a temptation – almost an obligation – to try to draw conclusions from the story of the raid. But what is there to draw? No more than has already been concluded, many times: that war brings fearful waste, of young men in their prime, of excellent machinery, of energy and skill; that even well-laid plans, once brought in contact with the enemy, are liable to fail; that the truth about an action is never easy to perceive, through all the physical and mental fog of war.

Turn, then, to the questions. Some of these have not been answered, and perhaps they never will. Why, for instance, did the Bostons' timing differ from the plan? Why did 44's formation fly north of their course? Why were the Browning guns, inadequate as they were, so further prone to failure? What happened to the plan to reach the factory in the last light of the day? Why – perhaps a minor question, this, but worth the asking – why did John Nettleton, in his broadcast of 19th April, refer to Halle E2 as 'T-shaped', when it was (and still is) rectangular? In this context, it has to be reported that, according to the M.A.N. archives, the formation leader's bombs fell squarely on the forging shop E3, the similar but smaller building just north of the assembly-shed; it was two subsequent bomb-loads which either hit, or had damaging near-misses on, E2. Then the fundamental question: why were the Lancasters and their pilots, designed and trained respectively to fly high and fly at night, committed to so different a role, and on a mission to a target which the bomber chief's directive did not require him to attack? As to this, it is interesting, though probably irrelevant, to note that, for two months or so before the raid, a US Army Air Force general had been a guest at Harris's residence near Command HQ. General Ira Eaker was assigned to take command of the US 8th Air Force in Great Britain (once there was an 8th Air Force in Great Britain to command), and General 'Hap' Arnold, his superior, had sent him to High Wycombe to study bombing tactics with the RAF. He and the Air Marshal had already met, and got on well together, while Harris was in Washington, heading an RAF purchasing team, in 1941, so Eaker was glad to stay, and study, with a friend. Harris and his right-hand man, Air Vice-Marshal Robert Saundby, while making Eaker free of their experience, had also done their best to wash his brains, and their experience, which was of aeroplanes equipped with rudimentary bomb-sights and low calibre machine-guns, had turned their hearts and minds towards a strategy of plastering a target, in the dark, with as many bombs as could be carried by the force at their disposal. By these means, they had kept their losses down to levels which, however sickening, were not so punitive as those of early daylight raids, and had kept up an offensive which was rather more than just a gesture of defiance. Harris saw the maintenance and steady growth of this campaign as being the only way to win the war without

132

the fearful death-roll he remembered from the 1914-18 battlefields. 'Come in with us on this offensive,' had been his message over cocktails to the General, 'The more bombs we drop, the better chance we have of crippling the bastards' war effort.' But Eaker would not be persuaded, not even when the voice of Winston Churchill (who visited the Harris home from time to time) had been brought in to join the serenade. Eaker's Flying Fortresses and Liberators would fly by day and, with the Norden bomb-sight, which defied the bombardiers to miss a pickle-barrel from whatever altitude they chose (or so they claimed), would spray no bombs around among the civil population but hit the vital targets on the nose. That was to be the USAAF way to prosecute the war. Harris had shrugged his shoulders, and continued planning to pour bombs down on Essen, Hamburg and Cologne, and one day soon upon Berlin, from every bomber he could get into the air. Churchill himself, when Eaker had suggested that their strategy should be to give the Nazis no relief by night or day, but to bomb them round the clock, had rolled the phrase around his tongue: 'Round-the-clock bombing,' he had growled, and nodded his approval.

Eaker opened his offensive in August 1942. From then until the end of the year, his sixty-odd Flying Fortresses flew some thirty missions with minimal losses – less than two per cent – and prodigious success (or so their gunners claimed) in shooting down the opposition. Strangely, the fact that, in achieving these results, no 8th Air Force bomber had yet bombed a German inland target, did not seem to qualify the great impression which they made on men who might have been expected to know better – the men whose job it was to run the bomber war. Even Air Marshal Harris was so moved as to write, abberatively, perhaps, or for some inner reason of his own, to the AOC 4 Group on 11 December 1942 in these terms: 'I think everybody is much too apprehensive about daylight operations . . .I have never been apprehensive about the ability of the bomber to look after itself in daylight vis-à-vis the fighter . . .It has long been our experience that whenever the rear gunner, even at night, sees the enemy fighter first, he either destroys it or the fighter refuses to come in and attack.' The gunners of Nettleton's formation, had they been able, might have taken leave to differ on that point.

In fact, the Allied bomber fleets would continue to pursue their complementary, if separate, campaigns: the RAF, gradually to gain in strength and, with the coming of new radar aids to navigation and the Pathfinders of 8 Group to mark the targets with their flares, to waste fewer bombs on open fields: the Americans in great formations, with the sunlight glinting on their wings, to venture ever deeper into Europe once the Thunderbolts and Mustangs could escort them on their way.

But that was for a later time – the time for reaping Harris's grim whirlwind. In April 1942, the facts of life were these: the further bombers had to fly to reach a German target, the fewer would come home: in daylight, fewer still. So in trying to visualise what might have persuaded Harris to despatch his Lancasters on the sort of mission of which Eaker only dreamed, and against the sort of target whose advocates he was accustomed to dismiss as 'panacea-mongers', the imagination conjures up a conversation-piece between the bomber chiefs. 'All right, Ira,' Harris says, 'so you're set on fighting your way through in daylight. I suppose you realise that four days out of five your boys will never see their target? North Europe isn't like Texas, you know.'

'Okay,' says Eaker, 'So we bring the bombs back and try again next day.'

'And you'll be restricted to targets inside the range of your fighter cover, unless you want to lose a lot of bombers.'

'Sure, Arthur,' Eaker agrees, 'We're counting on your Spits to go along with us as far as they can. But we believe we have some pretty good defensive formation tactics worked out to see us the rest of the way . . .'

'Look here, Ira, the only way to reach a German target in daylight would be at very low level – under the weather, under the RDF and the heavy flak, and making it damned hard for the fighters to get down amongst you . . .' Harris pauses, sipping his drink reflectively.

'I can understand why you feel that way, Arthur, but we do happen to have a bomb-sight that is extremely accurate from the B17's operational altitude . . .Arthur, you're not listening to me!'

'Of course I am, Ira. I was just thinking of something else. Now, you're sure the real reason you won't come in with us isn't because your chaps can't fly in the dark?'

But that is all in the imagination – nothing more. It is no answer to the question. Possibly the questions only serve to illustrate the last conclusion – that the truth is hard to find. It may be best to let the questions rest: the answers, if we had them, could never change the one truth that is clear and unassailable, that splendid airmanship was shown, and bravery, and monumental fortitude, by those who flew from Waddington and

Woodhall Spa on 17th April 1942. That is a conclusion to be carried forward, like a credit balance in the ledger of our times, and a truth to be remembered as the story ends.

Epilogue

With the ending of the story comes the hope that war itself will end. We have ideals, and principles, that we may think worth fighting for, but simplicity and clarity of thought might lead to other answers. When Erika Harbacher, an Augsburg child in 1942, was asked (perhaps a little pompously) how she had felt about the raid upon her town – upon that ancient caravanserai along the Romance Road, that focus of enlightenment and centre of the arts – she answered simply and clearly enough. 'I don't know about all that,' she said, 'it was just my home.'

GLOSSARY

AOC	Air Officer Commanding
'88'	German 8.8 cm Flak 36 heavy gun, usually in batteries of 4, firing an 18lb shell
ASI	Air Speed Indicator
ETA	Estimated Time of Arrival
Feldwebel	Rank equivalent to Sergeant
Fix	Aircraft's position as established by the navigator from an observed bearing or bearings
Flak	Fliegerabwehrkannonen – anti-aircraft fire
'Fulmina Regis Iusta'	No 44 Squadron Motto – 'The Thunderbolts of the King are righteous'
'Funnels'	Point on the circuit where the Drem lights funnel in to the flarepath
'Freya'	German surveillance radar
'Gee'	British aid to navigation. Three ground stations radiate pulses which appear on a receiver in the aircraft: measurement of the difference in their arrival time, when related to a special chart, gives the aircraft's position

'Gen Man'	One up-to-date with 'General Information' – well-informed, expert.
GP	General Purpose (bomb)
Geschwader	Luftwaffe formation approximating to an RAF Group, deploying 100 to 120 aircraft, and comprising three or four Gruppen. A Gruppe approximated to a Squadron, and comprised three or four Staffeln (Flights) each with nine aircraft, plus a Stab (Staff) unit with three aircraft
Gruppe	See Geschwader
Hauptmann	Rank equivalent to Flight Lieutenant
HCU	Heavy Conversion Unit
HE	High Explosive
IFF	Radio transmiter in aircraft for 'Identification, Friend or Foe'
Jagdgeschwader	German day fighter unit (see Geschwader)
Number Two, etc	In a V-shaped formation of 3 aircraft, the leader is No 1, the pilot on his right No 2, on his left No 3
OR	Operational Research
PT(I)	Physical Training (Instructor)
RDF	Radio Direction Finding
RNVR	Royal Naval Volunteer Reserve
RT	Radio Telephony
Second Dickey	Second Pilot
Staffel	See Geschwader

Staffel	See Geschwader
Unteroffizier	Rank equivalent to Corporal
u/s	Unserviceable
u/t	Under training
WOP/AG	Wireless Operator/Air Gunner
WT	Wireless Telegraphy

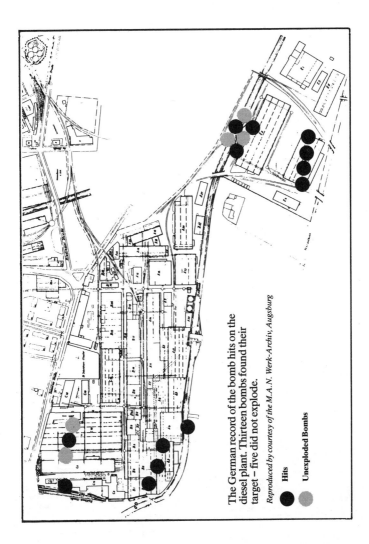

The German record of the bomb hits on the diesel plant. Thirteen bombs found their target – five did not explode.

Reproduced by courtesy of the M.A.N. Werk-Archiv, Augsburg

Hits

Unexploded Bombs

AIR 2 - 5686

Acting Squadron Leader John Dering NETTLETON, (41452),
No.44 (Rhodesia) Squadron.

Operational flying hours 96; Operational sorties 16.

Squadron Leader John Seymour SHERWOOD, (39132), D.F.C.
and Bar, No.97 Squadron.(Missing).

Operational flying hours 253; Operational sorties 43.

Each of the above officers led a formation of six Lancaster
heavy bombers in a low level attack on the Diesel Engine Factory
at Augsberg on the afternoon of 17th April, 1942.

1.   The formation led by Squadron Leader Nettleton was attacked by
25f30 fighters shortly after entering enemy occupied territory and
while flying at 50 feet.   A running fight ensued and his aircraft
were shot down one after another until only one remained to continue
the operation with him.   Early in this fight the guns of his rear
turret went out of action.   Nevertheless, he held on his course
towards his objective, which was known to be very strongly defended.

2.   After some 5 hours of strenuous and difficult low level flying,
he led the one remaining aircraft of his formation in the face of
most intense and accurate anti-aircraft fire at point blank range
in a determined attack on the target from just above roof-top height.
After both had discharged their bombs, the other aircraft burst into
flames and crash-landed on the outskirts of the target.   The bombs
of both aircraft were seen to explode amongst the factory buildings.

3.   With his aircraft riddled by shrapnel and his rear guns useless,
Squadron Leader Nettleton brought his aircraft and crew safely back
to base, over 400 miles of hostile territory.   The officer, who
already has a distinguished record of successfully completed
operations of a hazardous character against the enemy, showed in
this action the finest qualities of skilled airmanship, leadership,
courage and determination.

1.   Squadron Leader Sherwood led his formation with great skill
and ability at very low level across 900 miles of enemy occupied
territory, eventually leading all his aircraft directly on to the
target.   On the approach to the target itself, heavy and accurate
anti-aircraft fire was experienced, but, with extreme daring and
coolness, he pressed home the attack, scoring direct hits on the
factory with his bombs from a very low level.

2.   While bombing the target, Squadron Leader Sherwood's aircraft
was hit by anti-aircraft shells and caught fire.   He continued to
lead the formation away from the target with one wing well alight,
until the aircraft became uncontrollable.

3.   By extreme devotion to duty, Squadron Leader Sherwood ensured
the success of the operation with which he was charged, and continued
his daring leadership to the end.   His conspicuous bravery on this
occasion crowned a long and distinguished career in the service of
his country.

RECOMMENDATION FOR AN IMMEDIATE AWARD.

Khmced for award
final publicher...

Christian Names .John .Seymour .... Surname ..... SHERWOOD ....

Rank . Squadron. Leader .... Official Number ....

Command or Group . No..5. Group..... Unit ...97 Squadron..............

Total hours flown on operations . 253. hrs . 55. mins. ......

Number of sorties carried out ....43..............

Recognition for which recommended .....V.C..............

Appointment held..... Squadron Leader ....

Particulars of meritorious service for which the recommendation is made, including date and place.

Squadron Leader Sherwood, D.F.C. led his squadron on the daylight attack on the important Diesel Engine Factory at Augsberg, Southern Germany. With great skill and ability Squadron Leader Sherwood led the formation at very low level across 900 miles of enemy occupied territory - eventually leading all his aircraft directly on to the target. On the approach to the target itself, heavy and accurate anti-aircraft fire was experienced but, with extreme daring and cool-headedness, he pressed home the attack with his Section, scoring direct hits on the Factory with his bombs from a very low level.

While bombing the target his aircraft was hit by anti-aircraft guns and caught fire. Squadron Leader Sherwood continued to lead his section away from the target with one wing well alight and until such time as the aircraft became uncontrollable.

By extreme devotion to duty, Squadron Leader Sherwood ensured the success of the operation with which he was charged, and continued his daring leadership to the end. His conspicuous bravery on this occasion crowned a long and distinguished career in the service of his country.

Date 19th April,1942....

....
Signature of Commanding Officer.

Rank ....

Remarks by Air or other Officer Commanding:

This gallant leadership deserves the highest recognition. His example will always be remembered in this Group and in the Royal Air Force.

Date .19th April,1942...

....
Rank ....

Strongly recommend Cmdg No 5 Group
A.T. Harris AM
10/1/42

Other titles from Goodalls

LANCASTER TARGET

LANCASTER TARGET, the story of a RAF Bomber Command crew's tour of operations over Germany, enthrallingly told by Squadron Leader Jack Currie, DFC, was prominently featured in the BBC TV documentary, 'The Lancaster Legend', winner of the Royal Television Society Regional Television Programme Award, 1980.

UK £2.50   ISBN 0 907579 00 0

LANCASTER TO BERLIN

As its title implies this book by Canadian Pathfinder pilot, Walter Thompson, DFC and Bar concentrates on Bomber Command's 1943–44 offensive against the 'Big City' and the reader is taken in great detail through the drama of the great raids, from take-off to touchdown, a taste of what the crews had to face en route and over the target areas – flak, the risk of collision, the enemy night fighters . . .

UK £2.50   ISBN 0 907579 04 3

REAR GUNNER PATHFINDERS

Ron Smith DFM writes a vivid, action-packed story of 65 operations in the rear turret of a Lancaster, mainly with 156 Squadron of the Pathfinder Force. Foreword by Group Captain Hamish Mahaddie, DSO DFC AFC & Bar, one of the legendary Pathfinder commanders.

UK £2.50   ISBN 0 907579 02 7

ONLY OWLS AND BLOODY FOOLS FLY AT NIGHT

Group Captain Tom Sawyer DFC records five and a half wartime years with RAF Bomber Command from flying Whitleys in the early days to eventual command of No 51 Halifax Squadron and finally Station Commander successively at Burn, Driffield and Lissett.

UK £2.50   ISBN 0 907579 07 8

MOSQUITO VICTORY

This compelling, highly-readable sequel to Squadron Leader Jack Currie's best-seller LANCASTER TARGET describes the life of a RAF bomber pilot on 'rest' at an O.T.U. instructing trainees on the four-engined Halifax bomber, then later, on returning to operations, flying over enemy territory in Pathfinder Force Mosquitoes of 1409 Flight – the 'Weather Spies'.

UK £2.50   ISBN 0 907579 03 5

NO MOON TONIGHT

One of the greatest books ever written about Bomber Command – a classic of its kind. Don Charlwood, a wartime navigator with the Royal Australian Air Force, narrates a breathtakingly true story of a wartime bomber crew facing the hazards of bombing strongly-defended targets such as Essen, Dusseldorf, Duisburg, Nuremberg, Bremen, Berlin . . .

UK £2.50   ISBN 0 907579 06 X

ENEMY COAST AHEAD

Wing Commander Guy Gibson VC contributes what is widely regarded as one of the most brilliant and accurate descriptions of the raid by Lancaster of 617 Squadron – the Dam Busters – on the Moehne and Eder Dams which resulted in the flooding of the Ruhr Valley, heavily damaging the German war industry.

UK £2.50   ISBN 0 907579 08 6